IN GRATEFUL MEMORY

IN GRATEFUL MEMORY

The War Memorial
at North Kilworth

Dennis Edensor

DIAMOND D PUBLISHING
2009

Front cover: North Kilworth war memorial in 2005.
Rear cover: Princess Mary's gift box sent to E. W. Cheney at Christmas
1914. Frontispiece: The memorial shortly after it was dedicated in 1920
and before the railings were erected.

ISBN 0-9548400-1-1

First published in Great Britain 2009 by

DIAMOND D PUBLISHING
16 Avon Fields
Welford, Northampton NN6 6JL

Printed in England by Warwick Printing Company Limited, Leamington Spa

CONTENTS

FOR EVERMORE

THE memorial on the small green in the Leicestershire village of North Kilworth honours nine men, from private soldiers to a highly decorated brigadier general, who died in the First World War. Unusually, it also bears the names of fifty-nine men, and one woman, who served King and Country in 1914-18 but returned home. After the Second World War the names of a further four men, victims of that conflict, were added. On the memorial's cross is the familiar tribute Their Name Liveth For Evermore and the aim of this book is to help ensure that those seventy-three names should indeed endure as more than mere ciphers inscribed on stone panels. At the time of writing only five of the surnames on the memorial are still represented in North Kilworth. All the more important then that a record of the lives and service of villagers who went away to war should be compiled and so prevent the memorial from losing its meaning for later generations.

The First World War, intriguingly close, is yet tantalisingly remote. North Kilworth's last survivors have passed away long since and with them the chance to hear first-hand what it was like to be in uniform during those grim days. And, through modesty or perhaps sometimes a determination to bury unpleasant memories, those men of a no-fuss generation often fought shy of regaling their children with tales of wartime exploits. Family members, though anxious to help with this book, would apologise, 'Dad (or Grandad or Uncle) never said much about what he did in the war.' Also, although access to official records is much easier than it was, the amount of information available on individuals varies enormously. It means that in this book some men are the subject of reasonably complete biographies while others have entries running to only a few lines.

The scattering of village families across Britain and as far afield as France, the United States, Canada, Malta and New Zealand might have made it immensely difficult to trace relatives of some of the men, especially where surnames have changed through marriage. The knowledge of Rachel Root, of North Kilworth, was invaluable in this regard. She also provided photographs and family notes about life in the village in the first half of the twentieth century. Brian and Elaine Ball not only gave information about their family, which was profoundly affected by the Great War, but dug into their papers and albums to come up with pointers for further research. David and Liz Ward provided valuable help, particularly with information about the funding and erection of the memorial.

These relatives of men named on the memorial gave generously of their time and knowledge: Joan Ball, Robert Belgrave, Fay Brooks, Audrey Brookes, Terrance Brown, John Bozzoni, Les and Sheila Buckley, Jean and the late Peter Burbidge, Allen and Ethel Cheney, Jack Clarke, Barbara Coaton, Robert Cobbold, Anne Cullen, Mike and Val Dimblebee, Iris Dorman, Dinah Franklin, Esther Gudger, the late Ronald Hancock, Cynthia Hammond, Betty Harratt, Richard Haynes, Tom Hill, Michael Hinks, John and Joan Hollis, Marie Holyland, Michael Howkins, Irene Jones, Pat Kirk, the late Mary Lloyd, Rosemary McNeill, Eric Morris, Susan Murray, Denis Nash, George Nash, the late Joyce Nieland, Marjorie Petcher, Geoff Pitcher, David and Judy Price, Major General Charles Ramsay, Irene Scott, Peter Stapleton, the late Olwen Walton, David and Jacqueline Westcott, Kathleen Whelan, Evelyn Wickes and Rita Willis.

Others who were of great assistance include: Robert Constable-Maxwell, Harold Entwistle, Eveline Gandy, Peter Hughes, Olga Hutson, Stephen Lane, David Miller, Ruby Morley, Barbara Nightingale, Raymond Parfect, Isobel and Dennis Pepperill, Beryl Powis, Pam and Gwylim Price, the late Douglas Skene, Geoff Smith, and Bill and Nancy Thomas. John Mulholland's articles in *The Journal of The Victoria Cross Society,* edited by Brian Best, were most useful when it came to researching the story of Paul Kenna. Staff of the following institutions and organisations were unfailingly helpful: Commonwealth War Graves Commission, Eton College, Harrow School, Leicestershire And Rutland Family History Society and the museums of the Cheshire Regiment, Durham Light Infantry, Hampshire Regiment, Northamptonshire Regiment, Queen's Lancashire Regiment, Queen's Royal Lancers, Royal Welch Fusiliers and Staffordshire Regiment. Also the Army Museum, the RAF Museum, the public libraries of Market Harborough, Kettering and Rugby, the Oddfellows, the records offices of Leicestershire, Manchester, Norfolk and Warwickshire, Surrey History Centre, the National Archives, the Family Records Centre, London, Volksbund Deutsche Kriegsgräberfürsorge and the Library and Archives of Canada.

In the main, the photographs were supplied by relatives named above. The picture of Paul Kenna appears courtesy of the Queen's Royal Lancers Museum at Belvoir Castle. Special thanks are due to Clive Bradley for his work on the book's cover and the keys to group photographs. Adele Brearley gave technical assistance and Paul Hooper helped with genealogy. The diligence of Miles Hedley and Phil Todd in reading the text prevented several howlers. Errors that remain are, of course, the sole responsibility of the author.

Most importantly, heartfelt thanks to Jan, Gareth and James, who have had to live amid the ghosts of old soldiers for too long.

TO ARMAGEDDON

IT was a welcome fit for a hero. Villagers waiting at the country station raised a cheer, the brass band struck up a rousing tune; Harry Pallett, battle-seasoned sergeant of the mounted infantry, was back from the Boer War. The twenty-seven-year-old soldier who stepped from the train had been in South Africa from soon after the outbreak of hostilities more than two years before. He had taken part in the relief of besieged Kimberley, pursued the elusive enemy across the Orange Free State and helped put the Boers to flight at the battle of Diamond Hill. Enteric fever nearly killed him where Mauser bullets failed but now he was safely home in North Kilworth and everyone was determined to celebrate. Not even the weather could dull the mood that rainy Saturday, 28 December 1901. Henry Spiers, landlord of the White Lion, lent his wagonette to carry the sergeant the half mile from the station, accompanied by the band. As the sandy-haired soldier alighted in Back Street, at the cottage where his blacksmith father lived, the crowd gave three cheers for the King, the Army and Sergeant Pallett.

Residents were invited to contribute towards a gift for Kilworth's hero and the schoolroom was packed the following month for the presentation of a clock with an inscribed marble case. The Rector, the Reverend Cecil Cox, paid tribute to Pallett and all the nation's soldiers. He said that the war, which then still had four months to run, was a great calamity but had inspired extraordinary patriotism. The parson told his audience that if there had been an alliance against England by, say, France, Germany and Russia, as the Boers had hoped, there would have been not thousands but hundreds of thousands volunteering to take up arms in the country's defence. His speech was loudly applauded. Pallett thanked the villagers for the gift and kind wishes. His brother Thomas recalled how he was the last to see the soldier

Billy Pebody (far left) with friends at the washpit in about 1905

off at Southampton when he sailed to war and was the first to greet him when he landed back on his native shore. That was the cue for more applause before everyone trooped up to the White Lion where supper was laid on in the club room. George Ball, owner of the cart and implement works across the road from the pub, proposed a toast to the Army, Navy and Reserve Forces, coupled with the name of Sergeant Pallett. After more toasts the celebration was rounded off with a hearty sing-song.

The jolly crowd that dispersed into the darkness that winter's night could afford to indulge in its mild display of jingoism. Because the Boer War was fought and won, not by conscripts but by regulars such as Pallett, events could be followed, enjoyed even, by civilians safe at home as halfpenny newspapers devoted columns of dense type to developments on the veldt more than five thousand miles away. The songs of the war had an infectious music-hall vitality and the relief of Mafeking in May 1900 triggered wild rejoicing in the streets. (The school in North Kilworth jumped the gun by declaring a holiday on the strength of unconfirmed reports of the relief two days before official word reached London.) The war's toll of 5,774 men killed by enemy action or accident, while awful enough and much multiplied by deaths from disease, had a relatively limited impact on a population of forty-two million. One will look in vain in North Kilworth and most other villages for a memorial to victims of the Boer War.

The guests at the White Lion who so enthusiastically honoured a lone soldier could not have predicted that in fewer than thirteen years North Kilworth would start sending dozens of its sons into the most devastating conflict the world had seen. The national stampede to join up at the outbreak of the Great War in 1914 proved the Rector had been right when he expressed his confidence in men's readiness to serve their country in its time of need. But surely the toasts to plucky Pallett would have been more subdued had it been possible to foresee that a single day of the war, the opening of the Somme battle on 1 July 1916, would account for more than three times as many British deaths in action as the whole of the adventure in South Africa. Lads who scampered beside the sergeant's carriage on his ride from the station were among those fated to be sent to the Western Front. Pallett himself would serve in the Great War. Genial George Ball would see two sons off to war; one would never come back. Parson Cox was more fortunate. One son joined the army while another was decorated for gallantry at sea; both would see the old rectory again after peace was restored. Innkeeper Spiers's lad was also among those who did their stint and returned safely.

By the time the smoke of the guns cleared from a world irrevocably changed, the cost to North Kilworth would be nine men dead, at least ten wounded and others left with scarred minds to heal as best they could. Villagers who had contributed to Pallett's gift were again asked to dip into their pockets, this time to erect a memorial in honour of the fallen and the others who served – sixty-nine names in all. But this is jumping ahead of the story.

The village to which Harry Pallett returned early in the reign of Edward VII was home to about four hundred people. An agricultural depression in the nineteenth century had seen the population of North Kilworth decline a little and it would scarcely grow for another forty years. Despite that, the parish in the unspectacular, undulating country of south Leicestershire still provided rich pasture and good cereal-growing for farming families such as the Whitemans and Berridges, who had been there for generations. It meant jobs for shepherds, stockmen and general agricultural workers, although the pay was pitifully poor. There was also a modest living for independent graziers, who operated on a small scale and sometimes supplemented their income with other occupations. North Kilworth had its own mill on the Avon, reached along a track across the glebe pasture known as Stoney. At the village school it was expected that some of the forty-odd pupils would be absent to help at haymaking and harvest. As was typical in country areas of the early 1900s, villagers relied on oil-lamps to light their homes and hand-cranked pumps for their water. They would wait thirty years for electricity and fifty years for a mains water supply. Despite this essentially rural character, North Kilworth was no inaccessible backwater. At the London and North Western Railway station where Pallett was greeted trains departed for Rugby and Market Harborough with their main-line connections to London and the north. The stationmaster was Frederick Dilks, whose two boys would serve in the Great War.

A horse-drawn carrier's van operated from the village to Market Harborough on Tuesdays, Lutterworth on Thursdays and Leicester on Saturdays. Up the slight hill into Kilworth from the railway, the first inn reached was The Swan, where the host was former Life Guardsman Lancelot Holt. The White Lion was a few yards further west. The Howkins family had run the post office, next to the White Lion, for more than half a century and would continue to do so for another century. A son of the Howkins family would serve in the 1914-18 conflict. The village's third hostelry was the Shoulder of Mutton. Landlord William Packwood's grandson was another of the village's young men who would join up. In common with any sizeable village of the time, North Kilworth could supply the everyday needs of its residents without their having to travel. Butcher, baker, grocer, tailor and bootmaker were all in business. Widowed Elizabeth Wickes ran the bakery. Her grandson was to die in France in 1918.

St Andrew's church, known as St Clement's for some years in the 1900s, was a focus for social as well as spiritual life. (Non-conformists had had their own chapel since 1856; the nearest Roman Catholic church was at Husbands Bosworth two miles away.) Parson Cox, in office for only a few months at the time of Pallett's return, was the first Rector of North Kilworth for a virtually unbroken two hundred years who was not a member of the Belgrave family. When the Reverend Charles Belgrave, last of the line, died on Sunday 10 March 1901, less than seven weeks after Queen Victoria, it was as though North Kilworth had been robbed of two constants. Few could remember another monarch and only older residents recalled a rector other than kindly

North Kilworth's brass band with (rear from left) Charles Bennett, Arthur Whyles, Norman Maddison, Alf Pitcher, Charles Dunkley; (front) William Deacon, Harry Pitcher, Fred Allsopp, Herbert Allsopp, Harry Pebody and Ernest Sturgess

Charles Belgrave, who had officiated at the baptisms, marriages and funerals of villagers for forty-six years. The appointment of Cecil Cox was approved by the old Rector's nephew Colonel Dacres Belgrave, patron of the living and a principal landowner in the area. The Belgraves had held the local manor of Nether Hall since the early 1500s and owned property in North and South Kilworth before then. Dacres Belgrave's army career and later his other commitments kept him away from North Kilworth for much of the time. However it was the Colonel, by then aged seventy-two, who would be called upon in 1920 to unveil the village's war memorial. It was a particularly poignant duty for the old warrior; at the base of the stone cross the name of his own nephew was inscribed on the panel listing the fallen.

While the Belgrave family's roots in North Kilworth ran deep, in the early 1900s it was John and Mary Entwisle, relative newcomers, who played a more obvious part in village affairs. John Entwisle, son of a wealthy land-owning family from Rochdale in Lancashire, had moved to Leicestershire in the 1870s, married and had Kilworth House, in the parkland a mile west of North Kilworth, rebuilt as his home in an imposing style befitting a man of his status. He became a JP and High Sheriff of Leicestershire. Entwisle and his wife had no children but, to meet the domestic needs of the couple and various relatives often in residence, there were on average a dozen kitchen, scullery, laundry and house maids, a housekeeper, cook, two ladies' maids, four footmen and a hall boy. Bartlett the butler was custodian of a cellar which, at one stocktaking, contained fifteen gallons of casked whisky, dozens of bottles of fine port, seventy-five bottles of champagne, more than 280 bottles of claret and copious quantities of other wines and spirits.

The surrounding park and gardens and a magnificent conservatory stocked with geraniums, carnations, primulas, fuchsias and hydrangeas demanded the attention of the Scottish head gardener John Gauld, his three assistants and eight labourers. Kilworth's location on the fringe of the Pytchley Hunt's Wednesday country gave Entwisle, forty-three years old at the turn of the century, ample opportunity to indulge his passion for the chase. Wearing the white coat collar granted only to senior hunt members, he was a familiar sight in pursuit of a fox that had perhaps been flushed from a covert on his own land. His sporting interests meant employment for grooms who cared for the two hunters that shared stables with five horses for the Entwisles' brougham and Victoria carriages and dog-cart.

Wages on the estate were low; most of the female servants received less than ten shillings (50p) a week and the housekeeper drew a salary of sixty pounds a year. Few of the staff were from North Kilworth, although poor village girls, with little choice but to go into service, found positions in more modest households. The Entwisles, while paying their employees no more than the going rate, were generous enough when it came to the interests of the village as a whole. John Entwisle could be counted on to head the subscription list when a deserving cause needed a financial boost and his wife was a key figure in fund-raising social events. Typical of Mary Entwisle's gestures were the gift of a new altar cloth to the church in time for Christmas 1900 and the weekly supply of soup that she sent to the poorer cottagers each winter. Her husband provided gifts of coal for the widowed and aged poor and on one occasion also had a large number of rabbits, presumably taken from his land, distributed among parishioners. Yet status would not shield the couple from the tragedy of the Great War. John Entwisle's nephew was among the first to fall.

George Ball may have been overshadowed by the Entwisles in terms of wealth but he was every bit as prominent in village life. Still in his twenties as the new century dawned, the Governor, as he was known, ran a flourishing concern. The wagons, carts, floats and ploughs crafted by the family firm were of nationally renowned quality and won prizes at major agricultural shows, including the Royal, perhaps justifying the grand title Royal Implement Works emblazoned on the wall of the premises on the corner of the Lutterworth and Leicester roads. Further profit was made from undertaking and timber dealing. Shrewd Ball was the village's most important employer with about forty men on the books, including highly skilled wheelwrights, blacksmiths, farriers, carpenters and painters. When the Great War came the talents on which the firm thrived proved useful to an army still largely dependent on horse-drawn transport. (During the Boer War scores of horses were sent from North Kilworth to the Cape by the Heather brothers, dealers with stables in Back Street.) The workers who donned khaki included two of Ball's sons, one of whom, as already stated, failed to return.

The Governor could be relied on by local organisations needing practical support and he took on roles such as overseer for the parish council. John Entwisle had started an annual flower and vegetable show for North and South Kilworth in 1899 and from 1905 it was George Ball's energies as secretary that helped turn the event into an eagerly anticipated highlight of the social calendar. The exhibition, with a cricket match, athletic sports and sideshows contributing to the fete-like atmosphere, typified what has become the popular perception of life in Britain in the lead-up to the Great War. It was the glorious sunlit afternoon of prosperity, peace and innocence. The soft-focus image is of a country brightened by the example of a sport-loving King, but also one where respectful, God-fearing folk still doffed their caps to gentry who handed out prizes for the best displays of carrots and potatoes while elegant ladies wafted by and the band played. The cliché disguises a darker reality. It was also a time of poverty, political upheaval and industrial unrest. And of a tangle of international alliances and antagonism in which Britain became disastrously ensnared.

However, as Britain entered the Edwardian era, the clouds massing for Armageddon were still on the far horizon and certainly cast no shadow on North Kilworth. After the Boer War ended in May 1902 the country could concentrate on preparations for the first coronation in sixty-four years. The folk of North Kilworth, few of whom were ever likely to see their King, nevertheless relished the opportunity for a celebration. A committee was formed to decide how best to mark the occasion and forty pounds was raised by subscription. Coronation day was Thursday 26 June but news came through two days before that Edward had been struck by appendicitis and the ceremony would have to be postponed. Wednesday's newspapers announced that the King hoped celebrations across the country would go ahead and Kilworth was happy to comply. The school closed on the Wednesday for the weekend. Coronation day started at 8.30am with holy communion and the ringing of the church bells. There was a procession through the village, headed by South Wigston's brass band. Through a misunderstanding, the village's own band thought they would not be needed and had offered their services to nearby Welford instead. A hot dinner was

Football team (rear from left) Walter Morley, Jim Howkins, Tom Whiteman, Norman Maddison, Charles Dunkley, Herbert Bennett, Ted Hill, Frank Morley; (front) Arthur Whyles, Walter Sturgess, Bert Cheney, Ernest Spiers and Herbert Whyles

served for men and youths while women and children had to wait until afterwards for a meat tea. There was a sports afternoon and coronation mugs were distributed. Mrs Entwisle presented her specially ordered souvenirs – medals with red, white and blue ribbons for the schoolboys and brooches for the girls. The fun spilled over into Friday when beer, soft drinks and other refreshments were laid on.

Sidney Oxley was not born until a month after the coronation festivities and a couple of weeks before Edward had recovered sufficiently to be crowned on 9 August. Although only sixteen when the Great War ended in 1918, Oxley had joined the Royal Navy as a boy so his name would appear on the village memorial among those of the servicemen who survived. When Oxley was born, Paul Kenna was just short of his fortieth birthday and already held the Victoria Cross. Brigadier General Kenna, who had moved to North Kilworth a few years before the Great War, was killed in 1915 and his name was carved on the stone panel listing the fallen. Oxley and Kenna were the youngest and oldest men of the Great War honoured at Kilworth. What of the other sixty-seven names? About forty of the men named on the memorial were born in North Kilworth, mainly in the 1880s and 1890s; twenty-eight were baptised at St Andrew's. Among those was George Ball's son Victor, christened by Rector Belgrave in April 1897. The next infant taken to the font, a month later, was railwayman's son George Stock. The boys became schoolmates and both joined the army. Neither survived the war. Both Ball and Stock had brothers who were in the army but returned home safely. On the memorial there are another fourteen examples of brothers who served and several of the men named were linked through marriage.

At least thirty-six of the Great War men had attended the village school, built in 1847. Most of those were taught by Fanny Curry, headmistress from 1891 until early in the war. A photograph of some of Mrs Curry's young charges, taken in about 1907, features fourteen of the boys who would be in uniform a few years later. They include Victor Ball, George Stock and a third lad destined to die in the war, Sydney Wickes. Former pupils who faced the perils of active service had already survived the outbreaks of measles, scarlet fever and diphtheria that were an inevitable risk of childhood. More welcome aspects of the school calendar were the choosing of a queen and king each May Day and the arrival of a Christmas tree, courtesy of Mrs Entwisle, who also provided an orange, bun and useful gift for each scholar. And on winter mornings when the Pytchley met outside the White Lion the children were allowed out of lessons to see the hounds.

Pupils could hardly fail to assimilate the notion of King, Country and Empire watched over by an approving God. Trafalgar Day on 21 October was recognised with suitable lessons and the late Queen's birthday was marked as Empire Day each 24 May. When, one year, the children sent an exhibit to the flower show it seemed obvious that it should be in the form of the Union Flag. Patriotic parson Cox went into school each morning to give a scripture lesson, as had his predecessor. Many pupils also attended the Sunday school and each year youngsters from both schools were treated to tea at the rectory where they received prizes before taking over Tom Whiteman's orchard for games. The Entwisles took a particular interest in the schools and would invite the youngsters to tea on the lawns at Kilworth House, where the gardeners put up see-saws and swings. Away from adult supervision local lads gathered at the washpit or played ball in a field near the White Lion where gipsies camped and small fairs were sometimes held.

Children who started school at age four or earlier stayed until they were about thirteen when they could take the tests for the labour certificate which released them into the world of work. For most, this transition into adult life meant long hours of toil and a level of pay allowing for few luxuries. But there were simple, inexpensive pleasures to brighten the weekly grind. The village had an enthusiastic football club with the Rector, a keen athlete in his youth, as president. Jim Howkins, from the post office, was secretary and treasurer and future soldiers in the team included him, Alf Stapleton, Percy Hill, Ball's workers Charlie Dunkley, Frank and Walter Morley, Bert Cheney and Ernie Spiers and gardener Arthur Whyles. In 1902-03, its first season in the Rugby and District League, the side was defeated only twice, beating even the champions BTH, who recruited players from among the hundreds of workers at the British Thomson-Houston electrical engineering works in Rugby. There was also a village cricket team whose fixtures included a friendly against John Entwisle's staff XI on flower show day. Arthur Whyles was for years the team's driving force.

An air rifle club was formed in North Kilworth in 1906. Such clubs were encouraged as they were seen as a way to give young men at least some experience of handling weapons in a country where conscription was taboo.

Whyles, Dunkley and Hill, along with Frank and Jack Knight, George Morris and Frank Morley, were among the enthusiastic marksmen who would take up arms more seriously in the Great War. The club practised twice a week, became affiliated to the National Air Rifle Association and shot some closely contested matches with rivals from Husbands Bosworth and South Kilworth. A boxing club formed around the same time did not flourish to the same extent.

The focal point for entertainment in Edwardian times was the Belgrave Memorial Hall, built to honour the memory of the late Rector. John Entwisle presided over the committee set up to fund the building and Colonel Belgrave provided a site at the foot of Church Street. George Ball, with another prominent villager, Thomas Clarke, supervised the building contract and a tender for £142 was accepted from a Kettering firm of builders that had George Phillips, a native of Kilworth, as one of its partners. Mrs Entwisle opened the building on the evening of 5 January 1903, three months after laying the foundation stone. The inevitable speeches were followed by a concert then the floor was cleared for dancing into the early hours. Villagers were soon making good use of their new hall, organising dances, whist drives, bazaars and jumble sales for causes such as church maintenance. A concert and dance held each January to mark the anniversary of the hall's opening were guaranteed a good attendance.

Away from business, George Ball loved entertaining and was always ready to play his banjo or impersonate music hall singer and comedian Harry Lauder. One of the greatest attractions, however, was the village's minstrel troupe whose members used burnt cork to 'black up' for performances that were taken as great fun at the time but might offend today. The leading roles of Tambo and Bones were usually taken by Ball and wheelwright Alf Phillips respectively and Fred Hill, a railway clerk, was among those who acted as Interlocutor or master of ceremonies. There was even a junior troupe, drilled by Phillips and Mrs Curry. Each Christmas the brass band, whose members included Arthur Whyles, Charlie Dunkley – those game lads again – and another future soldier, Harry Pebody, toured the village to play carols and other seasonal tunes. Hand-bell ringers also performed outside homes from which they could generally expect a festive tip.

These parochial scenes were played out to a backdrop of national events which, although of far-reaching importance, sometimes seemed of little direct

North Kilworth school about 1907. Fourteen of the boys pictured are named on the war memorial

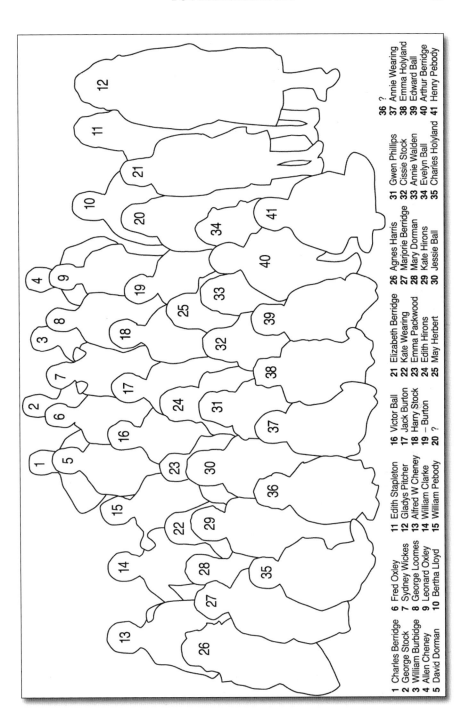

1 Charles Berridge
2 George Stock
3 William Burbidge
4 Allen Cheney
5 David Dorman

6 Fred Oxley
7 Sydney Wickes
8 George Loomes
9 Leonard Oxley
10 Bertha Lloyd

11 Edith Stapleton
12 Gladys Pitcher
13 Alfred W Cheney
14 William Clarke
15 William Pebody

16 Victor Ball
17 Jack Burton
18 Harry Stock
19 – Burton
20 ?

21 Elizabeth Berridge
22 Kate Wearing
23 Emma Packwood
24 Edith Hirons
25 May Herbert

26 Agnes Harris
27 Marjorie Berridge
28 Mary Dorman
29 Kate Hirons
30 Jessie Ball

31 Gwen Phillips
32 Cissie Stock
33 Annie Walden
34 Evelyn Ball
35 Charles Holyland

36 ?
37 Annie Wearing
38 Emma Holyland
39 Edward Ball
40 Arthur Berridge
41 Henry Pebody

concern to villagers. Mounting labour troubles from 1910 to 1912, including strikes on the railways and in the cotton mills, docks and coal mines, scarcely touched a community remote from industrial centres. Also, the motoring age was gathering momentum but pony-drawn traps and grooms leading Pytchley hunters to shoeing were more likely to be encountered in the village than cars, the preserve of the well-off. George Ball had one of the first motors locally, a single-cylinder De Dion Bouton with no reverse gear. John Entwisle's first car, a twenty-eight horsepower Lanchester, was delivered new in July 1909. It seated six including the driver. A coachman and some of the stable staff at Kilworth House made way for a chauffeur and garage hands.

Of more significance to workers in North Kilworth were welfare changes pushed through by the Liberal Chancellor David Lloyd George in 1911. Previously any villager unable to earn through long-term illness had to fall back on meagre savings and any cash forthcoming from a local charity, sickness clubs, family and neighbours. Some evenings of fun at the Belgrave Memorial Hall had the serious purpose of raising a few pounds for a local person fallen on hard times. The new National Insurance Act required working people to pay to insure against sickness. Contributions were based on the actuarial figures of the Oddfellows, which had become the world's largest and richest friendly society in the nineteenth century. The Oddfellows and similar organisations were appointed as 'approved societies' to administer national insurance on behalf of the state. Many new Oddfellows branches, or lodges, were opened, including in 1912 the Belgrave Lodge No 8718 in North Kilworth. By the Great War the lodge had thirty-one members and £789 in funds. Lodge nights, held every fourth Tuesday in the schoolroom, were social occasions as well as the opportunity to collect subscriptions. There was also a ceremonial element and each Whitsun lodge members paraded through the village behind their banner before a church service and celebratory meal at the White Lion.

Edward VII did not live long enough to see the introduction of the welfare reforms which would benefit the British people with whom he was so popular. Aged fifty-nine when he became King, Edward had ruled for only nine years when he died on 6 May 1910. North Kilworth's arrangements for the coronation of George V on 22 June 1911 were broadly a re-run of the celebrations to mark the crowning of his father. The school closed for the week and, two days before the big day, Mrs Entwisle invited pupils, teachers and forty mothers to Kilworth House where tea was served on a terrace festooned with flags and bunting. The tables were covered with fruit, cake, flowers and decorations shaped like gold crowns. There were games on the lawn and boating on the lake. On coronation day the village awoke at 5.30am to a peal of the church bells. A pole on the green was decorated with flags and the schoolchildren followed the brass band to church for a special service. There was then a procession through the village before a hot lunch was served for men and boys aged over fourteen. Women and younger children were again segregated and had to wait until 4pm for their meat tea. The celebrations continued with a baby show, tug-of-war and sports and all children under twelve received a coronation mug.

As the bunting was taken down there remained a little over three years before the outbreak of the war that would see George V rebranding his largely Germanic family as the House of Windsor. It is outside the scope of this book to explore the origins of the Great War in detail. Edward VII had charmed the old enemy France on a visit to Paris in 1903, paving the way for an entente cordiale. Meanwhile Edward's petulant nephew Wilhelm, the German Kaiser, seemed never quite sure whether to love or hate his uncle's country. The Kaiser rejoiced in his honorary British rank as Admiral of the Fleet. Yet he revelled in Germany's race to send new battleships down the slipways at a rate to challenge the supremacy of the Royal Navy. Britain responded with its own massively expensive programme of building Dreadnoughts and battlecruisers. Germany, Austria-Hungary and Italy renewed their Triple Alliance in 1907. Soon afterwards Britain sealed an understanding with Russia aimed at eliminating friction between their empires in the Middle East and Central Asia. Germany claimed to fear encirclement as France and Russia were already formal allies. It was a mountain of unstable explosive awaiting ignition.

Two pistol shots provided the spark. On 28 June 1914 Archduke Franz Ferdinand, heir to the Austro-Hungarian empire, and his wife Sophie were assassinated by Bosnian Serb gunman Gavrilo Princip. Austria, egged on by Germany, blamed Serbia for the outrage and declared war on 28 July. The Russian Tsar Nicholas II, honour-bound to defend fellow Slavs, ordered mobilisation. Yet, as the August bank holiday weekend approached – it was early in the month in those days – Britain clung to the hope that a full-blown European war could be averted.

Bosnia, Serbia, Russia; all must have seemed far away to the folk of North Kilworth as they looked forward to the village's sixteenth annual flower and vegetable show on Saturday 1 August. The event had been moved four years previously from the grounds of Kilworth House to the more conveniently situated paddocks of Tom Whiteman and Charles Holyland, who was by then landlord of the Shoulder of Mutton. Poor weather meant fewer people than usual were there to admire the exhibits and enjoy the band, comedian, sports, skittle competitions and other amusements. By the time the stalls were cleared that evening Germany had declared war on Russia. Germany declared war on France on the Monday and defied Britain's ultimatum not to send its troops through neutral Belgium. At 11pm on Tuesday 4 August Britain declared war.

The following Saturday's *Rugby Advertiser* devoted much of its second page to the flower show and printed a comprehensive list of prize winners. On the opposite page, given similar prominence, was a report under the headline THE GREAT CONTINENTAL WAR. As readers studied the details of both events the effects of the conflict were already starting to be felt in North Kilworth.

WAR AND REMEMBRANCE

K ITCHENER needed recruits – lots of them and quickly. North Kilworth, like the rest of Britain, was ready to answer his call. Field Marshal Earl Kitchener, premier soldier of the Empire and newly appointed Secretary of State for War, declared that the conflict would last three years and need a million troops, estimates that astounded the politicians but would prove hopelessly optimistic. Britain relied on the Royal Navy to protect the Empire and homeland and its volunteer army was tiny by comparison with those of France and Germany. Kitchener called for the first hundred thousand volunteers and by the end of August had very nearly three times that number. The iconic Kitchener poster proclaiming Your Country Needs You had not gone to the printers when Bert Cheney, a wheelwright at Ball's, joined up a week after war was declared. Charlie Carter, a painter at the firm, followed less than four weeks later. Albert Clarke, a baker at the village's Co-op, volunteered the day after Carter.

They were not the first in uniform. Pals George Ball Jnr, Ted Cheney (no relation to Bert) and Walter Morley, who all worked for George's father, had joined the Leicestershire Yeomanry the previous year. The Yeomanry, cavalry of the Territorial Force, provided a taste of military life for young men prepared to devote some leisure time to training and annual camp. A recruit signed only to say he was available for home defence duties in the event of war; there was no commitment to serve abroad. However, when hostilities did come most men agreed to go. On the first weekend of the war Morley, Cheney and young Ball were waved off with their comrades from Lutterworth station to the accompaniment of cheers, tears and the town band. They were in Belgium by early November. George Jnr's younger brother Victor and blacksmith Fred Pallett, brother of Boer War veteran Harry, also joined up at some stage. Harry himself, pensioned off from the army earlier in 1914, was welcomed back by his old regiment, the Cheshires. Brigadier General Kenna and John Entwisle's nephew Captain Meyricke Lloyd, as professional officers, were already with their regiments when war was declared.

Nationally, there were many reasons behind the rush to join up. An escape from the drudgery of mine or factory was often an incentive. For some men the prospect of three square meals a day and regular pay was enough. Kilworth's early volunteers, like so many others, probably acted through a mix of impulse, simple patriotism, the lure of adventure and the chance to have a go at 'the Huns' over their treatment of 'plucky little Belgium'. Among Ball's workers there was perhaps an element of pals egging on each other. One suspects that the Governor's pride in his employees' readiness to serve their country was diluted by concern about the impact of their absence on his business, especially when more joined up later.

While the young men of North Kilworth enlisted, or at least considered doing so, the women were also determined to contribute to the war effort. At Kilworth House Mrs Entwisle had the servants raid the linen store for surplus woollen and cotton materials to be turned into garments for soldiers in France. Women from the village were drafted in to help with the sewing and parcels were sent off in early September.

By then the British Expeditionary Force had retreated in relatively good order from the Belgian town of Mons and, with the French, held the German advance at the River Marne. There followed the so-called race to the sea with each side trying to outflank the other until the Channel coast was reached and the conflict bogged down in the trench warfare that would dominate the next four years. Although 1,186,357 men were to volunteer by the end of the year, more were needed. Meetings aimed at persuading or shaming ditherers to sign up were held all over the country. Typical was a public meeting at the Belgrave Memorial Hall in October. Parson Cox presided as members of the Leicestershire Recruiting Committee made their pitch. Many men and women attended and joined in the patriotic songs. However, reminders of the perils facing any young man persuaded to join up were not long in coming. Towards the end of October the Entwisles received the news that Meyricke Lloyd had died of wounds during the first battle of Ypres, the Flemish town whose name would become synonymous with the horror of the Great War. It is no slight on Captain Lloyd to say his death was felt less acutely in the village than at Kilworth House. As a career officer, he visited his aunt and uncle at Kilworth infrequently and had little reason to mix in ordinary village life.

Mark Hampson was also a professional soldier. He had married Annie Neale, daughter of a North Kilworth family, while he was serving in South Africa and she was there working for a doctor. On Wednesday 4 November the long-serving colour sergeant was killed in the little-remembered battle for Tanga, a port in German East Africa. Like Lloyd, Hampson was not well known in Kilworth if indeed he was ever a visitor there. However, the two soldiers' connections with the village assured their places on a memorial then still undreamt of.

The hope of an end to hostilities by Christmas soon evaporated. Thoughts turned to letting those at the front know they were not forgotten over the festive season. On the initiative of Princess Mary, the King's seventeen-year-old daughter, a fund was launched to send a present 'from the whole nation to every sailor afloat and every soldier at the front'. The gifts were embossed brass boxes, each containing a Christmas card and photograph of the Princess along with tobacco and cigarettes or chocolate. North Kilworth sent its own presents to each village man. Cash was raised to dispatch parcels containing a woollen cardigan, a quarter-pound tin of chocolate powder, a tin of sardines, two packets of cigarettes, three pairs of bootlaces, peppermints, notepaper, envelopes and an indelible pencil.

The new year promised only further bloodshed; efforts in 1915 to break the deadlock on the Western Front were to prove costly and ineffective. That March North Kilworth lost another man, wagoner's son Albert Spriggs, who died of wounds in the Ypres salient. Growing casualty lists in the first quarter of 1915 did not deter another three Ball employees from joining the army. They were George Morris, Charlie Dunkley and Frank Morley, younger brother of Walter who had gone with the Yeomanry. All were family men. Given the uncertain future such volunteers faced, they probably felt entitled to one or two farewell drinks before departing for service and people thought it natural to stand them a round to wish them good luck. Not everyone approved of the custom, though. That February the Church of England Temperance Society held a meeting at North Kilworth school where the Rector proposed a resolution, unanimously passed, calling for an end to

Fete at North Kilworth on 30 August 1919. Mrs Whiteman holds her presentation tea service

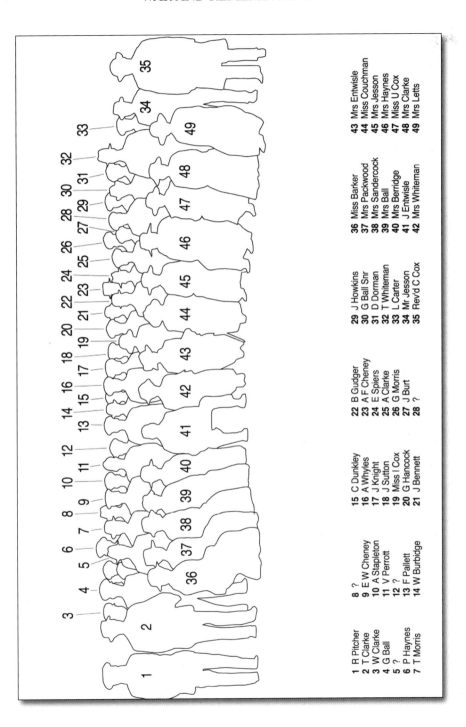

1 R Pitcher
2 T Clarke
3 W Clarke
4 G Ball
5 ?
6 P Haynes
7 T Morris
8 ?
9 E W Cheney
10 A Stapleton
11 V Perrott
12 ?
13 F Pallett
14 W Burbidge
15 C Dunkley
16 A Whyles
17 J Knight
18 J Sutton
19 Miss I Cox
20 G Hancock
21 J Bennett
22 B Gudger
23 A F Cheney
24 E Spiers
25 A Clarke
26 G Morris
27 J Burt
28 ?
29 J Howkins
30 G Ball Snr
31 D Dorman
32 T Whiteman
33 L Carter
34 Mr Jesson
35 Rev'd C Cox
36 Miss Barker
37 Mrs Packwood
38 Mrs Sandercock
39 Mrs Ball
40 Mrs Berridge
41 J Entwisle
42 Mrs Whiteman
43 Mrs Entwisle
44 Miss Couchman
45 Mrs Jesson
46 Mrs Haynes
47 Miss U Cox
48 Mrs Clarke
49 Mrs Letts

'treating' because it led to drunkenness. 'Such a manner of saying farewell to the brave men who come forward to defend this country is unpatriotic,' the clergyman declared. George Ball was more relaxed about booze. There is a story that the Governor provided a barrel of beer later in the war when some of his former workers each happened to be home on leave at the same time. The pals are said to have downed the ale in the firm's paint shop before lurching home the worse for wear.

The women at home continued to do what they could. Miss Ramsay, a relation of the Entwisles staying at Kilworth House, helped organise a collection of eggs to be sent each Tuesday to a central depot in London where the Red Cross distributed them to hospitals caring for sick and wounded soldiers. Kilworth's Boy Scout troop, formed in 1913, delivered the eggs to the village station. Local women with sons and husbands serving in France lived in constant anxiety, especially after Charlic Carter and fellow volunteer Will Burbidge were wounded early in 1915. But on 1 July they were able to push their worries to the back of their minds for an hour or two when Mrs Entwisle invited them and their families and friends to tea on the terrace at Kilworth House. Afterwards the guests strolled through the grounds, boated on the lake and danced to tunes from a Pianola.

Entries for the annual flower and vegetable show the following month were said to be 'well up to the average' despite several of the regular exhibitors being away at war. Brigadier General Kenna who, before promotion from Colonel, was a member of the show's organising committee and had judged the sports in 1912 and 1913, could not be there; he was in Gallipoli, commanding his brigade as part of the Allies' ill-fated attempt to take the Turkish peninsula. On 30 August 1915, a couple of couple of weeks after the Kilworth show, Kenna died, shot by a sniper. He would be the highest ranking soldier, as well as the oldest, named on the memorial at North Kilworth. September 1915 brought another attempt at a breakthrough on the Western Front. At Loos in the coalfields of northern France the British launched a costly battle for only meagre gains. About this time wounded soldiers recuperating in hospital at Lutterworth were entertained to tea at North Kilworth rectory. George Ball collected and returned some of the guests in his motor. The sight of such casualties was a reminder of the pressing need for yet more volunteers to fill the gaps among the troops at the front, but through the summer and autumn of 1915 voluntary enlistment slumped. Lord Derby was made Director General of Recruiting in the October. Under his Derby Scheme all men between the ages of eighteen and forty-one were urged to attest in the knowledge that they would not be called up until actually needed. In North Kilworth the parish council was asked to form a recruiting committee. At a meeting on 10 November a list of names for the committee was drawn up to be sent to the co-ordinating offices in Leicester. The Derby Scheme was of limited success but by the time it closed in December several more North Kilworth men had taken the oath.

One more village family was in mourning before the end of 1915. John Dorman was serving with the army in France when he died of appendicitis on 2 December. Although he had married and settled in Rugby before the war he would be deemed a son of Kilworth when the village memorial was erected. The war was less than half way through and five names of the dead were already awaiting commemoration.

With 1916 came the inevitable introduction of conscription and at least seven more North Kilworth men were in uniform before the end of March. As the army of civilian soldiers grew so did hopes that 1916 would be Britain's year of triumph. It was not to be. Urged on by the French, the British agreed to join in a Big Push. At 7.30am on 1 July, a beautiful summer's day, the infantry climbed from trenches along an eighteen-mile front north of the River Somme. Men were told to expect scant opposition because of the one and a half million shells fired into the enemy lines in a week-long bombardment. However, the Germans, largely unscathed, emerged from superbly constructed dug-outs in time to man their machine-guns. Swathes of British were mown down trying to reach gaps in the enemy wire, which the shelling had largely failed to cut. At the end of the first day of the Battle of the Somme there were 57,470 British casualties. Of those, 19,240 were killed. By the time the battle petered out in the November snow more than 95,000 British soldiers had died.

In some towns several homes in a single street lost a husband or son. Yet North Kilworth was spared; not one man from the village died during the whole of 1916. Yet there was a sombre air to the place. By the end of the year most of the young men were away in uniform and any approaching the age of eighteen knew that they, too, would be called up before long with the prospect of active service abroad when they reached nineteen. The horticultural show was not held in 1916 and it would be 1925 before it was

The fete, 30 August 1919: (rear from left) A. Pitcher, J. Knight, T. Morris, W. Burbidge, P. Haynes, A. Clarke, G. Hancock, H. Sharp, J. Howkins, J. Sutton, D. Dorman, A. F. Cheney (partly hidden), C. Carter, J. Bennett, J. Dorman, A. W. Cheney, E. Spiers, W. Pebody, L. Carter, ?; (front) C. Dunkley, G. Morris, A. Stapleton, G. Ball, I. Cox, W. Clarke, F. Pallett, E. W. Cheney, A. Whyles resurrected. People at home continued to do what little they could to help or comfort victims of the war. Typical of North Kilworth's efforts in 1916 was a slide show of Rocky Mountain scenes held to raise funds for blinded soldiers. After Christmas the village lost one of the driving forces behind charitable endeavours when Mary Entwisle died at the age of fifty-seven.

With 1917 came hopes of new vigour in the approach to the war. Herbert Asquith, ageing and demoralised, had been replaced as Prime Minister by the dynamic David Lloyd George. Fresh offensives were to be launched on the Western Front, inevitably meaning lengthening casualty lists. But young North Kilworth railwayman George Stock had not even left Britain when he died on 16 February. He was still at an army training camp in Staffordshire as he fell victim to influenza. The fact that he never had chance to see action would not prevent him being honoured on the memorial when the time came.

By then farmer Tom Whiteman's wife had become the champion of North Kilworth's servicemen. Indefatigable Edith Whiteman, known by her second name Minnie, was herself a farmer's daughter from Desborough and had moved to Kilworth on her marriage in 1910 when she was twenty-seven. Despite having two young children, Mrs Whiteman organised weekly work sessions at the farm in Back Street where she was joined by other women knitting scarves and gloves for the soldiers. She gave the helpers tea afterwards. A whist drive was held in the Belgrave Memorial Hall on 22 October 1917 to raise funds to send Christmas parcels to the servicemen, who by then numbered nearly forty. Local people provided the prizes, such as game, fowl and home-made jam. A social and dance was held the following evening for the same cause.

Civilians were feeling the effects of the war; bread rationing was imposed as the Germans conducted unrestricted submarine warfare against cargo vessels. North Kilworth's schoolchildren were encouraged to gather chestnuts and were even given a half holiday in October to pick blackberries for jam-making as a small contribution towards easing shortages. Eggs were still being collected for dispatch to the Red Cross.

As 1916 will be seared forever on the British consciousness as the year of the Somme, so 1917 was the year of Passchendaele, although there were other important battles. Images of shell-stripped skeletons of trees and fatigued Tommies picking their way along duckboards through a sea of mud during what was officially called the Third Battle of Ypres are seen, misleadingly, as typical of the Great War. The infantry attack began on 31 July and by the time the offensive was called off in November the net gain was four and a half miles of ground, the losses an estimated seventy thousand Allied dead and more than two hundred thousand other casualties. On the slope below Passchendaele Ridge is Tyne Cot, the largest Commonwealth War Graves Commission cemetery in the world. There are twelve thousand graves – yet no man from North Kilworth lies there. The village was not directly affected by the hell of Third Ypres. It would not be so fortunate in the coming year.

No one knew if 1918 would bring victory or even an end to the war. It brought both, along with the highest number of casualties of any year of the conflict. As an indication of how desperate the army was for men, village lad George Buswell was hardly past his eighteenth birthday when he went into the army in mid-February. That month the people of North Kilworth were given a novel opportunity to see the enemy at first hand when about forty German prisoners of war were brought to work on the land. They were accommodated in stables at the Hawthorns, a large house on the green. The prisoners 'are a small type of men and comprise Germans, Prussians and Bavarians', the *Rugby Advertiser* noted. Village children were warned to ignore the arrivals, who leaned from windows to try to talk to them. Soon after the prisoners had settled in, a party of them paraded under guard to the church for a Sunday service. Catholics among the Germans were marched to Husbands Bosworth for a service of their own.

On Thursday 21 March the prisoners' comrades on the Western Front took part in the start of Germany's last great offensive. It was the final throw of the dice, an onslaught that, had it been successful, would have pushed Britain and France out of the war. The previous Friday forty registered envelopes, each containing 3s 6d (17.5p) as an Easter gift, had been dispatched by Mrs Whiteman and her helpers to the village's servicemen, the money having been raised at a whist drive. For nineteen-year-old soldier Sydney Wickes the gesture came too late. As specially trained shock troops led the German attacks on the first day of the offensive he was killed near Arras. His envelope, returned to Mrs Whiteman from France, always remained among her papers, a sad reminder of the war's toll. Another envelope containing five shillings (25p) was sent to a prisoner of war,

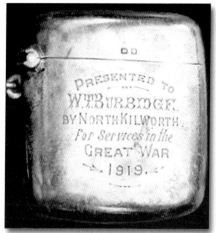
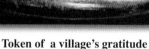

Token of a village's gratitude   **Another of the 59 matchboxes**

possibly Will Cheney, who had been wounded and captured the previous year. He would be released under exchange arrangements before the war's end. Within a day or so of Wickes's death Victor Ball was also taken prisoner. James Howkins and Horace Sharp were the other North Kilworth men who became PoWs.

The situation in France became grave as British troops were driven back, yielding ground won at terrible cost. However the Germans lacked the reserves and supplies to consolidate their gains and morale among their exhausted soldiers started to suffer. The war was still in the balance on 13 June when Colonel Belgrave's nephew James, a Royal Flying Corps pilot, was killed. He crashed while diving in pursuit of a German aircraft. Although James Belgrave was not well known in North Kilworth, his family's centuries-long connection with the village would guarantee his name being on the memorial. Six days after Belgrave was killed Victor Ball died in captivity in circumstances never explained. His family did not receive confirmation of his death until after the war. Now there were nine names of the fallen to be honoured. There would be no more. In August the tide of war had turned and allied troops, bolstered by the arrival of US soldiers, forced the Germans into a final retreat. The Armistice came on Monday 11 November. In North Kilworth flags flew all week, bonfires were lit and on the Friday the church bells rang for a thanksgiving service.

The bishop conducting the service at the dedication of North Kilworth's memorial on 18 April 1920

One hesitates to express grief and loss in simple terms of arithmetic. However, it is perhaps of interest to see how North Kilworth fared in the Great War compared with the country as a whole. About one in ten of the total number of British troops mobilised during the war died. The figure for Kilworth is about one in eight as nine of the sixty-nine names on the memorial are of men who died. It is one in eleven if James Belgrave, Mark Hampson and Meyricke Lloyd are discounted as being not strictly of the village. Whatever formula is applied, North Kilworth's men more than paid their dues and, with the coming of peace, the village resolved that their service and sacrifice should not be forgotten.

A committee of local folk decided that a war memorial should be erected on the green and that a gift costing about one pound should be given to each returning soldier and sailor at a reception in their honour. In May 1919 J. G. Pullen & Sons, masons of Bridge Street, Northampton, sent a list of possible designs for the memorial. At a meeting of the committee on 27 June a choice of a cross and base was confirmed. The committee also agreed that the servicemen's gifts should take the form of suitably inscribed silver matchboxes. It is no surprise that the task of raising the necessary funds fell largely on Minnie Whiteman who, during the war, had shown such skill in coaxing donations from people for the presents sent to the servicemen. Now, as secretary and treasurer of the committee, she succeeded in finding more than 120 subscribers. John Entwisle headed the list with a donation of twenty-five pounds. The Rector gave ten pounds, as did Colonel Belgrave, George Ball, Tom Whiteman and fellow farmer James Haynes. Many subscribers gave five shillings (25p) or half a crown (12.5p). Even gifts as little as threepence (1.25p) were welcomed. Supplemented by more than twenty-five pounds from whist drives and dances, the fund that Mrs Whiteman kept in the post office eventually topped £212.

The reception, with a fete, was staged on Saturday 30 August 1919. Many of the war veterans who attended were in uniform. George Ball Jnr and William Clarke, in particular, were immaculate in their officers' outfits. Other men were in their best civilian suits and stylish caps or bowler hats. It is uncertain how many attended but photographs show about thirty present. The men formed up at the post office and Wigston United Prize Brass Band led them in procession to the Whitemans' paddock. There were sports and Will Eagle's concert party from Kettering provided entertainment. The band played during the afternoon and struck up again in the evening for dancing. A meat tea was laid on for the servicemen and there were speeches from Colonel Belgrave, John Entwisle, the Rector, Tom Whiteman and others. Towards the end of the event each man was presented with his matchbox by the new Mrs Entwisle. Widowed John Entwisle had married Florence, daughter of his cousin Sir Alexander Ramsay, four months earlier. Each box bore the words: Presented To – By North Kilworth For Services in the Great War 1919. (At least eight of the boxes, with flip-up lids and rings for attachment to a chain, are known to be still in the hands of the recipients' families.) The Whitemans' little daughter Mabel presented a bouquet to Mrs Entwistle and a silver-topped toilet bottle to Irene Cox, the Rector's daughter, who had served in some capacity during the war. Miss Cox then handed Mrs Whiteman an engraved silver Queen Anne tea service and tray, a surprise gift from the servicemen in appreciation of her efforts on their behalf. As dusk fell on a highly successful day the ground was lit with fairy lamps.

The event left Mrs Whiteman with a pile of bills to settle. Charles Holyland at the Shoulder of Mutton had supplied an eighteen-gallon barrel of India pale ale and a two-dozen case of spruce (soft drink), and the White Lion was owed for two dozen bottles of ginger beer. There were accounts for 250 corona light cigars, two hundred bread cobs, forty-five pounds of ham, thirty-six pounds of tinned beef, other meat plus currant and plain cakes. The band charged £7 10s (£7.50). The greatest expense was the men's gifts. George Allen, jewellers in Market Harborough, charged twenty-two shillings (£1.10) each for fifty-nine matchboxes and seventeen shillings (85p) for Miss Cox's toilet bottle, engraving included.

By then plans for the memorial were finalised. The organising committee had studied pictures from Pullen's of at least thirty possible types of cross, each available with various bases and steps. Model H was selected, a cross in Weldon stone on an octagonal base. Overall it rises about 13ft 6in from ground level and the steps of Derbyshire stone on which it stands are about seven feet across and rest on a concrete foundation. Lutterworth Rural District Council granted the necessary approval in the June. When the clerk Thomas Bodycote wrote to Mrs Whiteman to tell her of the decision he added, 'I congratulate you upon your selection of so beautiful a design.' There was some indecision about whether iron railings to enclose the site, some twelve feet across, should be on a square or octagonal plan. The latter was eventually chosen. The words Their Name Liveth For Evermore were carved into the stone at the bottom of the cross. Inscribed on one of the eight tablets of the base was the tribute: To The Glory Of God And In Memory Of The Men From This Parish Who Fell In The Great War 1914-1919. The next panel bore the names of the fallen in order of rank:

BRIG. GEN. P. A. KENNA
V.C. D.S.O. A.D.C.
CAPT. J. D. BELGRAVE M.C.
CAPT. M. E. LLOYD
SERGT. M. HAMPSON
PTE. V. E. BALL
PTE. J. T. DORMAN
PTE. A. SPRIGGS
PTE. G. W. STOCK
PTE. S. W. WICKES

The third panel carried the words: Also In Thankful Appreciation Of The Services Of The Men From This Parish Who Served Their King And Country. On the remaining five panels were the sixty names of those who returned, twelve names to each panel, in alphabetical order. It is fairly unusual to find a memorial that lists survivors but other local examples include the ones at Gumley and at East Farndon. Pullen's charged £112 to supply and erect the memorial, £10 18s 9d (£10.94) to cut and black the inscriptions, at three shillings (15p) for every dozen characters, and £34 5s (£34.25) for the 3ft 6in iron railings with a gate and lock, although the committee decided the gate should remain unsecured.

The railings were not erected until after the memorial was dedicated on 18 April 1920 by the Bishop of Peterborough Frank Woods. It was a fine spring Sunday. There was a short prayer at the church then at 3pm a procession wound its way to the green. With a cross held aloft, the choir, churchwardens and sidesmen led the way, followed by the men who had served or their representatives. Then came the bishop and other clergy and a large congregation singing *Onward, Christian Soldiers*. The Rector conducted the first part of the service and the lesson was read by Mr Plumbridge, the Congregational minister, who took as his text ten verses from Ephesians with their martial references to the 'whole armour of God' and 'sword of the Spirit'. The congregation sang the hymn *O God, Our Help in Ages Past* to the accompaniment of the Pebody family's harmonium played by the Rector's elder daughter Ursula Cox. Colonel Belgrave then unveiled the panels of the memorial. The bishop dedicated the cross, saying it would always be a consecrated spot in the middle of the village. The ceremony closed with everyone singing the National Anthem and a collection was taken for blinded sailors and soldiers. At some stage a North Kilworth roll of honour, hand-scribed in blue, red and gold, was also produced. It hangs inside St Andrew's on the south wall.

In October 1920 the committee paid Pullen's £3 15s (£3.75) for two stone vases as an adornment for the memorial. Those who had spent such time and care ensuring that the village properly honoured its fallen never foresaw that within twenty-five years another world war would have been fought, meaning space had to be found for more names. It would entail changing two of the panels to accommodate the new inscriptions. The result is that the names of the Great War fallen appear on the memorial today without rank and in alphabetical order. That is how they are listed in the next chapter.

THE FALLEN

V. E. BALL

THE first story from the war memorial is one of the most poignant. Victor Ball, born into a prosperous family, might have expected a long and fulfilling life, perhaps playing an important role in his father's business. The Great War meant that was not to be.

Having joined the cavalry only to be transferred to the infantry, Victor was captured by the Germans in 1918. His postcards home from a prisoner-of-war camp soon ceased and his increasingly worried family's letters to him went unanswered. When the war ended the Balls were still left without word of Victor's fate. His former girlfriend, who had broken off their relationship before his capture, was stricken with remorse. She wrote to the soldier's mother in the early days of peace in an attempt to explain her feelings. Neither woman knew that Victor, by then, had been dead for months. Victor's father explored every avenue to discover what had become of his son but it was months before it was finally confirmed that Victor had died in captivity. Even then the Balls' efforts to discover the circumstances of his death were cruelly frustrated. Victor's grieving parents never learned how he lost his life.

Victor Ernest Ball was the second son of George William Ball, the Governor, who figures prominently in the previous chapters. George was born in 1872 in Rothwell, Northamptonshire, where the family firm of William Ball and Son, agricultural implement makers, was based. George's father had died suddenly five days before he was born so his mother took her child to live at North Kilworth, where an uncle ran a similar operation. George was apprenticed as a wheelwright and eventually took over the

Kilworth business, which flourished under his leadership. In September 1895 George married Maria Atkins, a labourer's daughter, at Wigston church. He was twenty-two, she was twenty-one. Their first son George Jnr was born the following year. Victor was born on 3 March 1897 and baptised by Rector Charles Belgrave on 18 April. The Balls were to have three more sons and three daughters.

Victor joined the infants' class at the village school on 9 March 1900, the same day as William Cheney, who was also destined to become a prisoner of the Germans. In 1905, when he was eight, Victor won the fifty-yards race for younger boys at the annual summer flower show. He was a willing scholar as well as budding athlete. In 1908 he won a school prize for the best attendance with 417 sessions out of a possible 420. Victor's record a couple of years previously was marred slightly when he was absent for the day after swallowing a halfpenny. More seriously, in 1910 he and three siblings had to be kept home when their family was stricken with highly contagious diphtheria. In September that year Victor left to attend Lutterworth Grammar School.

At the outbreak of war in August 1914, Victor was still only seventeen and working for his father. George Jnr immediately left for war service with the Leicestershire Yeomanry. Victor enlisted at Rothwell but his service records have not survived so the date is unknown. He followed his brother into the cavalry and became Private 23537 in the 17th (Duke of Cambridge's Own) Lancers. Photographs of him proud in uniform show the 17th's famous badge, or motto as it is styled, of a skull and crossed bones, with the words 'Or Glory' below. The regiment, stationed in India since 1905, had sailed to France in October 1914 as part of the 1st Indian Cavalry Division. However, it was obvious that racing headlong on horseback into enemy gun positions would have made even less sense in 1914-18 than it had in 1854 when the 17th Lancers were in the first line of the Charge of the Light Brigade. Many cavalrymen were switched to an infantry role and young Ball was transferred at some stage to The Queen's (Royal West Surrey) Regiment, second most senior infantry regiment of the British Army. Now Private G/22090, he was posted to the 7th (Service) Battalion, which had been formed at Guildford in September 1914 as part of K2, the second of the armies raised from volunteers who responded to Kitchener's call to arms at the outbreak of war. The battalion went to France in July 1915. However, as it is known that

Victor Ball with 17th Lancers' Death Or Glory badge on his cap

Victor Ball found that his cavalryman's skills were little needed

Victor did not qualify for the 1914 Star or 1914-15 Star, it seems he did not enter a war zone until 1916 at the earliest. In March 1918 he was with the battalion in the Somme region nine or ten miles south of St Quentin and squarely in the path of the great German spring offensive that was about to be launched. Mid-month the battalion was relieved in the front line by the 7th Buffs and moved back a little to the village of Liez where it worked improving strong points and wire defences and establishing dumps of rations, water and ammunition. At 11pm on 20 March orders were received that an enemy assault was anticipated in the morning. The Germans started intense shelling at 4.45am and the battalion took up battle positions. As the heavy dawn mist cleared it became obvious that the Germans had broken through on either flank. The Surreys were involved in fighting on their right flank and a patrol sent out to reach the Buffs was captured by the Germans. A counter-attack involving the Surreys was being contemplated when the order came through to withdraw over the St Quentin Canal a kilometre or so to the west. The move started at 4am on the 22nd and that evening the battalion was in position ready to support any move against the enemy. The following day the battalion, hampered by mist and fog, was badly mauled by the Germans. Over the next few days the remnants of the battalion moved back, stage by stage, over ground won at such appalling cost in the Somme offensive of 1916.

Ball was not with his retreating comrades. He had been captured on 22 March and taken the short distance to a prisoner-of-war camp at Flavy-le-Martel. As any mail he sent home had to go via a central camp at Stendal in Germany, there was inevitably a delay in his family learning of his capture. On 22 April 1918 Victor's mother wrote to him of everyday family matters, saying, 'We do feel so anxious about you, it is over a month now since I heard from you.' Mrs Ball wrote again on 1 May, signing herself 'Your anxious mother'. The family had by then heard that Victor was missing and his mother wrote, 'I do hope you are safe somewhere. I feel you must be as I have had no letters returned.' She included the news that Victor's brother George was to be married on 14 May. Finally, to the family's immense relief, a pencilled postcard dated 5 April arrived. Victor, concerned to break the news of his capture as gently as possible, first made a mundane reference to his wellbeing. He wrote, 'Dear Mar, At last I have the pleasure of writing to let you know I am fairly well, bar a bit of a cold. Well you will see by the card

I am a prisoner of war, was taken on the 22nd. I have no address at present so take no notice of that other address on the opposite side (a reference to details on the French postcard he had scrounged to send his message). With love to ALL, Your Loving Son. Victor.'

The captured soldier wrote again, on an official German form, to say he was still fairly well and asked his mother to send him cigarettes. Mrs Ball replied on 18 June to let her son know his cards were arriving and that she was sending him a photo of George's wedding. 'We are all well at home,' she wrote. 'Hoping this will find you the same.' Victor never read the letter. He died in the camp the day after his mother wrote it. The records show that the twenty-one-year-old soldier died at 11.30pm on Wednesday the 19th but there is no indication of cause. Unaware of her loss, Mrs Ball continued to send letters and parcels to her son. On 2 August she wrote, 'I have not heard from you for a month. I am feeling rather anxious about you.' Later that month Victor's twenty-year-old sister Evelyn also wrote, telling him that fellow prisoner Will Cheney had been freed and was in a London hospital.

On 16 October, another of Victor's sisters, seventeen-year-old Jessie, sent a letter only hinting at the constant agonies of uncertainty that now racked the family. She wrote, 'We had a dance here last night, the room was absolutely packed. I've never seen it so full for a long time. The money is to pay for the parcels that are sent out to you and Mr Howkins. You two are the only prisoners from the village now. Horace Sharpe and Willie Cheney have been exchanged. We haven't heard from you for quite a long time, hope we shall get a letter through soon. Will close now, with best love from all, your everloving sister Jess x.'

Jessie enclosed a letter for Victor, posted in August by his old pal, stationmaster's son Fred Dilks, who appears to have been serving in India. Fred said he knew Victor was a prisoner but added, 'With good luck we shall meet at the Staff Of Life again.' The Staff Of Life, a pub at Mowsley four miles from Kilworth, was not far from Saddington Reservoir where George Ball had fishing rights and took his family for relaxation. Fred also told Victor he had heard that he had been dropped by his girlfriend and made the inevitable comment about there being 'more than one fish in the sea'. He promised his friend a game of cribbage 'in about 1927, or later', adding, 'With the good news we are getting from France it might finish a bit before that, so don't worry.'

Despite the war ending in November, the Balls still had no word about Victor. They could only cling to hope and badger the authorities for information. Victor's former girlfriend, who was called Madge and lived in Plowman Street, Rugby, was moved to write to his mother. The letter from a girl who, of course, had no way of knowing that her former sweetheart had died five months previously, is extremely touching. Madge wrote, 'Dear Mrs Ball, I expect you will be very much surprised to hear from me, but now that Peace has come I feel I must write. I hope you have heard from Victor by now. Please Mrs Ball don't think it was through me that Victor was taken prisoner, I am truly sorry he was taken. I have been very unhappy since I given (sic) him up, but I expect that is a little punishment for my wrongdoing. I hope that before long poor Victor will be restored to you. I have prayed every night and asked God to keep him safe. I hope that you will

Madge, Victor Ball's girlfriend

one day forgive me, and that Victor will soon be home. I will now close hoping you are feeling better and not thinking too badly of me. Yours sincerely, Madge.'

George Ball, increasingly frustrated and fearful, made determined attempts to discover his son's fate. The Prisoners of War Relief Fund run by Victor's regiment could offer little in response to Ball's appeal for help in

January 1919. Fund officials promised to ask still-returning prisoners if they knew anything and posted up Victor's name in the Guildford barracks with a request for information. Impatient at the lack of progress, George travelled to London to call at the Infantry Record Office in London but to no avail. He also wrote to the *Daily Mail* after reading an article on Our Missing In Germany. In early February Ball received a letter he had dreaded. The Central Prisoners of War Committee, organised by the British Red Cross, wrote to say of Victor, 'It is more than probable that he did not survive his captivity.' Officials promised to send Victor's name to Berlin in an attempt to find out more. The War Office also wrote to say Victor's name would be sent to the German authorities in the list of prisoners who, although not known to be dead, had not been repatriated. As late as July the British Military Mission in Berlin wrote to Ball asking for details to aid the search for his son. It is difficult to imagine the anguish caused in the family by a letter sent from the War Office on 5 August stating that Victor had died in the camp at Flavy-le-Martel and giving the time and date nearly fourteen months before. Victor, the Balls were told, was buried in Grave No 376 at Cugny military cemetery, a mile or two from Flavy.

In January of 1920 George Ball received £26 16s 7d (£26.83), the pay and war gratuity due to his son. The following month the War Office sent on Victor's personal effects, received from Germany. The Balls' grief was not allowed to ease. In January 1921 they were notified that Victor's body had been exhumed to be re-interred at Grand Seraucourt British Cemetery, south west of St Quentin. It was part of a tidying-up of the former battlefields to move bodies from small, inconveniently situated burial grounds and scattered graves into larger concentration cemeteries.

George Ball, with no idea whether his son had died of illness or for some reason more sinister, wrote to Infantry Records in 1921 to request more information. He was told in the August that it had not been possible to trace any soldier who was in the camp at the time of Victor's death. Ball received his son's British War Medal and Victory Medal in the post shortly afterwards. The mystery of Victor's death has never been solved. Today he rests at Grand Seraucourt in grave VI F 5.

J. D. BELGRAVE

IN the spring of 1914 James Dacres Belgrave was still at public school. By the end of the year he was an infantry officer preparing to be sent to the Western Front. He had yet to turn nineteen when he was wounded and gassed at Loos in 1915. Belgrave transferred to the Royal Flying Corps, became a fighter ace and was decorated twice for bravery before he was killed in action in the summer of 1918. He was still only twenty-one. His story underlines how, for young men of the 'officer class' in the Great War, status brought disproportionate risk and, very often, death.

Belgrave was not born in North Kilworth nor was he even a frequent visitor; but it was where his roots lay. His grandfather Thomas was son of one of the village's long line of Belgrave rectors. Thomas became a commander in the Royal Navy and his wife Charlotte was a daughter of Vice-Admiral James Richard Dacres, a hero of the War of 1812. There started a tradition of Belgrave sons being christened in honour of gallant Dacres, which explains James's distinctive second name. James's father Dalrymple was Commander Belgrave's younger son. Dalrymple went to Cambridge, became a barrister and, demonstrating an adventurous streak, set up a legal practice in the South African diamond boom town of Kimberley in 1880. When he returned to England a few years later he wrote books based on the characters he had encountered. In 1894 Dalrymple married Isabella Richardson, whose forebears belonged to a network of Quaker entrepreneurs and bankers in the north-east of England. By the 1890s Isabella's widowed mother was living in Switzerland and Dalrymple and Isabella were married in January 1894 at Territet on Lake Geneva. Their first son Charles was born in Switzerland that December. The couple moved to London in time for James to be born at their house in Pitt Street, a few minutes' stroll from Kensington Palace, on 27 September 1896.

Charles and James started as day boys at their father's old school, Bedford Grammar, in November 1905. James made no great impact academically and his chief sporting achievement was a place in the successful Second VIII rowing squad of 1913. He was in the school's cadet corps and was set on a career in the army. There was no shortage of military influences; his uncle Dacres, who by then held the family estate at North Kilworth, had retired as a lieutenant colonel and Dacres's two sons were forging distinguished army careers. James left the sixth form in the summer of 1914 as war loomed and was rushed through the Royal Military College at Sandhurst. On 16 December 1914, less than three months after his 18th birthday, James passed out of Sandhurst and was welcomed as a second lieutenant in the Oxfordshire and Buckinghamshire Light Infantry. This was effectively his local regiment as his parents had by then moved to the Oxfordshire village of Chinnor.

Belgrave was initially posted to the 3rd (Special Reserve) Battalion at Portsmouth but on 31 May 1915 he joined the 2nd Battalion in France where it had suffered heavy casualties in the Battle of Festubert. He found the battalion in trenches at the mining village of Mazingarbe between Béthune and Lens. This was not the Western Front of flooded shell craters and knee-deep mud; Belgrave was greeted by cloying heat and a dazzling glare from the chalk soil. Mosquitoes were as much a nuisance as German snipers. Belgrave, allocated to D Company, settled into the routine whereby the battalion alternated with others between front-line positions and billets to the rear. Over the coming weeks there was a steady drip of casualties from enemy mortars and shells as the British prepared to launch a Big Push aimed at breaking the stalemate on the Western Front. It would become known as the Battle of Loos, after the mining town whose capture was a key objective.

On 23 September the Ox & Bucks took their place in trenches at Givenchy on the northern boundary of the main attack positions. The flat, open terrain was far from ideal for an infantry attack against an entrenched enemy but the generals hoped that the release of poison gas, being used for the first time by the British, would panic and disable the Germans. Unfortunately the wind failed to co-operate. When the attack was launched at 6am on 25 September the Ox & Bucks found that the gas was hardly moving or was even blowing back towards them. D Company faced withering machine-gun fire and Belgrave had hardly climbed from the trenches when he was caught by the blast of a high-explosive shell. Dozens of tiny fragments of metal and dirt peppered the right side of his face and he was half-buried by earth thrown up by the explosion. Barely conscious and deafened in his right ear, he started choking on the gas. Fortunately he was rescued without delay and taken for treatment. Further south, British troops made good gains; but the reserves were too far behind to exploit the successes and fend off counter-attacks. The breakthrough didn't happen and the Ox & Bucks' casualties for 25 September totalled eight officers and 270 other ranks.

James Belgrave after he was awarded the Military Cross in 1917

Belgrave was among the wounded taken back across the Channel on 27 September, his nineteenth birthday. He was sent on sick leave and his face wounds soon healed as he rested at Chinnor. Deafness, giddiness and faintness resulting from the shell blast also started to fade. He was promoted lieutenant on 13 February 1916 and rejoined his battalion in France on 2 June.

He was there only briefly as he had been accepted to train as a pilot with the Royal Flying Corps. That September he was sent to the Central Flying School at Upavon in Wiltshire. With less than three months' flying experience he was posted on 30 November to No 45 Squadron as it prepared to move to its new base at Ste-Marie-Cappel in the flat Flanders farmlands. The squadron flew the Sopwith One-and-a-Half Strutter, a sound enough biplane but hardly a match for the latest German scout machines. The two-seater Strutter had a single fixed Vickers machine-gun, which fired through the propeller and was operated by the pilot. An observer/gunner in the rear seat had a Lewis machine-gun on a moveable mount.

The Squadron had the tough dual role of flying photo-reconnaissance missions and tackling German aircraft that ventured over the Ypres salient. Belgrave did not encounter the enemy until Christmas Eve when he joined a four-aircraft patrol. North-east of Ypres he saw a German aircraft and dived towards it from 10,000ft. He opened fire but the German sped away to safety. Belgrave's engine then spluttered and died and he had to glide to a British aerodrome at Bailleul where he landed safely. Next day the war was temporarily forgotten as the officers and NCOs of No 45 Squadron followed seasonal tradition by serving the men their Christmas dinner. For Belgrave nothing much came of other sightings of the enemy until, on 7 February 1917, he scored his first victory and extricated a fellow pilot from a perilous situation into the bargain.

Belgrave was in one of four Strutters escorting a fifth machine that was photographing enemy positions. Four German single-seaters pounced on the formation, sending one aircraft to its doom. Belgrave chased a German Albatros and fired at it until it suddenly fell into a vertical dive, out of control. He then turned his attention to another German, who was circling in an attempt to stay on the tail of Captain Eric Lubbock's Sopwith. Belgrave's gun was out of ammunition but he manoeuvred into a position that allowed his observer John Thompson to empty a drum of Lewis bullets into the German at very close range. The enemy dived away and Lubbock was safe again.

Two days later Belgrave again saved Lubbock from being shot down. The two were chasing a German two-seater when two enemy scouts appeared. Belgrave opened fire, driving one away, then turned to rejoin Lubbock. It was lucky that he did because the other German had dived on Lubbock's aircraft just as his observer found his gun had jammed. Lubbock flung his aircraft into violent turns in an attempt to shake off his pursuer but the German followed every move. In desperation Lubbock put his aircraft into two loops. The Sopwith could not take the strain. Half of its tail folded back and Lubbock struggled frantically to maintain control as the aircraft went into a steep dive with the German still only feet behind. Belgrave followed the two down but was able to get in only two short bursts at the German for fear of hitting the Sopwith. However, his actions gave Lubbock's observer time to clear his gun and open fire at the German, who then turned away. Lubbock eased his crippled machine out of its dive, made a forced landing and climbed out unscathed.

In March Belgrave went on leave for two weeks. While he was away five close comrades, including Lubbock, were killed in action. Then, on Good Friday, 6 April, another six fliers of No 45 Squadron died. Belgrave refused to be deterred and on 5 May his courage and persistence were rewarded with his third victory. He spotted five or six enemy aircraft, tucked in under the tail of one of them and got in a long burst at close range. The German aircraft went into a spin, rolled over and fell away. Two days later Belgrave notched up his fourth victory when he and his patrol became entangled in a dogfight with six Germans. Belgrave dived firing on one Albatros, which burst into flames and went straight down.

On the evening of 24 May Belgrave became an ace – a pilot with five victories to his credit. He was on a patrol that met nine German scouts over Zonnebeke. Belgrave opened fire from close range on a German aircraft that was on the tail of another Sopwith and the enemy went into an out-of-control dive. Three days later he scored his sixth victory when he shot down an enemy attacking another Sopwith. Belgrave was sent home in July 1917 as word came through that he had been awarded the Military Cross for 'conspicuous gallantry and devotion to duty'.

The following month he was with No 61 (Home Defence) Squadron, flying Sopwith Pups and first-rate SE5a single-seaters from Rochford, now Southend Airport. His targets were the Zeppelin airships and Gotha and Giant bombers striking at London and other centres. In August he twice chased Gothas that

James Belgrave (front, third from right) at Bedford School

had attacked south coast towns but was unable to shoot any down. On 6 October Belgrave, now appointed a flight commander with the rank of temporary captain, was lucky to escape with his life in a flying accident. He was taking up a Pup to test its gun when he collided with an Avro at low level. He suffered a black eye and slight concussion but was fit for flying again within a few weeks. By April 1918 Belgrave was needed back on the Western Front. He joined No 60 Squadron, which was equipped with the SE5a, at Boffles, a remote aerodrome ten miles north-west of Doullens.

He was soon engaging enemy aircraft but it was 15 May before he opened his scoring for the squadron. As if to make up for lost time, he achieved a double victory. Belgrave was leading a twelve-aircraft formation east of Arras when he saw eighteen brightly coloured Albatros scouts. Despite the adverse odds, he turned to meet them. He fired at a purple Albatros then watched as the aircraft went into a corkscrew spin and crashed. Within five minutes he had climbed and fired at another Albatros, which went spinning out of control. Next morning he attacked a German two-seater reconnaissance machine, firing from such close range that he almost collided with it. Belgrave's guns then stopped and the German glided away to land in a field. Later in the day

Belgrave scored his ninth victory proper. He dived out of the sun and fired at two Albatros scouts. He left the first for another of his pilots to deal with but the second went into a vertical dive, emitting black smoke.

His tenth and eleventh victories came on 18 May when he downed a two-seater and, 15 minutes later, an Albatros scout. Belgrave's relentless attacking spirit inspired the Squadron's commanding officer Major Barry Moore to write to Wing headquarters, saying, 'Captain Belgrave as a patrol leader is magnificent, possessing the greatest initiative and showing utter fearlessness.' Belgrave scored his twelfth victory on 21 May when he shot down a German while other SE5as kept at bay four scouts intent on diving to the rescue of his victim.

Next day Belgrave got on the tail of a yellow Albatros and fired from only fifteen feet away. He saw his bullets hitting the fuselage and pilot of the enemy aircraft and narrowly avoided a collision as it fell to its destruction. More success came on 28 May when he shot at a two-seater which burst into flames and broke up. Belgrave was on patrol with only two other pilots on the evening of 5 June when, contemptuous of the odds, he went into battle against up to thirteen brightly coloured Fokker triplanes. It was a classic dogfight with planes jinking, dodging and zooming. Belgrave shot down a green triplane that crashed in flames then he broke off the fight to lead his patrol home as fuel was running short. On 9 June he chalked up his sixteenth and seventeenth victories, shooting down two Germans with the help of another member of his patrol. There had been several other, less decisive but nonetheless perilous encounters with the enemy in the previous weeks and Belgrave received word that his remorseless efforts had earned him a bar to his Military Cross.

His luck could not hold. At dawn on Thursday 13 June Belgrave took off from Boffles with three comrades to hunt German aircraft. After half an hour he saw an enemy two-seater and dived on it from 9,000ft. Belgrave, still chasing his prey, vanished into the ground mist about four miles east of the battered town of Albert. It seems he had scored his eighteenth victory because an anti-aircraft battery reported that the German aircraft crashed. But the gunners also saw a British machine go down behind enemy lines and Belgrave did not return from patrol. The Germans later dropped a message over the lines confirming that he had been killed. It was never explained whether he was shot down or simply hit the ground in bad visibility. Major Moore wrote to his parents to say, 'The lads would have followed your son anywhere.' The place where the Germans buried Belgrave was found after the Allies pushed eastwards and he was re-interred in Grove Town Cemetery at Méaulte, south of Albert. Belgrave is commemorated on the war memorial at Chinnor. However, it is hardly surprising that his name is also included on the memorial at Kilworth, given his family's long association with the village. The name of James's brother Charles (later Sir Charles) does not appear among those of the men who returned even though he served in the Royal Warwickshire Regiment and various camel corps. The family erected a fine brass plaque in St Andrew's in memory of James. It bears the inscription Thy Will Be Done, as does his grave, in plot III A 19 at Grove Town.

J. DORMAN

THREE Dorman sons donned uniform in the war; one of them never returned home. John Dorman, married with a boy aged two, died in France in 1915 and it was of little consolation to his family that he fell victim to illness rather than the enemy. John was the eldest son of William Thomas Dorman, a farm labourer whose own father, also John, was a Kilworth-born grazier with a couple of cows that supplied villagers with milk. In 1884 William, then twenty-six, married Sarah Jane Robinson, a twenty-seven-year-old servant whose family came from Newark in Nottinghamshire. The couple set up home in a cottage on the stretch of Rugby Road, North Kilworth, called Little London. William, or Tom as he was better known, was recalled many years later as a jovial character fond of a sing-song at the pub.

John Dorman was born on 27 November 1884 and christened John Thomas by Rector Belgrave almost a year later. He started at the village school in June 1888 before he was four. He appears not to have been a very willing scholar as the attendance officer issued a warning about his absences when he was nine. An earlier absence when the Dorman family was hit by measles was, of course, hardly his fault. In April 1896 John asked for a labour certificate to cease school, at the same time as another future soldier, Charles Dunkley. He started worked on the land, like his father, but later went to live in Rugby where he found a job as a groom. At the age of twenty-seven he married Rugby girl Mary Violet Hinks, two years his junior. The ceremony

John Dorman as an ambulance driver after joining up in 1915

was at St Peter's, Rugby, on 27 July 1912. The couple lived in Albert Street near the town centre and their son, named John after his father but called Jack in the family, was born in the summer of 1913.

The responsibilities of providing for a wife and baby perhaps made John immune to the initial war fever of 1914 but in May 1915 he went to the drill hall in Park Road, Rugby, and volunteered for the Army Service Corps. Within weeks he was driving ambulances in France. He was posted there as Private M2/099389 of the Corps' Mechanical Transport arm and was attached to 26th Field Ambulance, Royal Army Medical Corps. John's nineteen-year-old sister Mary went to stay with his wife in Albert Street while he was away and he wrote to her there on 1 August to thank her for a cake and other items she had sent him. 'I am keeping very fit and I am well and I hope you are the same,' he wrote. However, within a few months John was stricken with appendicitis. He died, aged thirty-one, on 2 December 1915 in the Canadian General Hospital at Etaples. The Dormans were one of many families mourning that Christmas. At least John's younger brothers, Joe and David, were to survive their service in the army.

John Dorman's name was already on the memorial in North Kilworth when names were being gathered for war memorial gates to be erected in Rugby. Perhaps his widow thought there might be objections to him being commemorated in two places but, for whatever reason, she appears not to have put his name forward until the last moment. However, when the gates were dedicated in March 1922, with Viscount French of Ypres present, John Dorman's name was among more than four hundred of the fallen listed on the panels. Unfortunately his name appeared as J. V. Dorman; perhaps some clerk, in his haste, had misheard T as V. Among the many wreaths left at the gates was one bearing the tribute 'Pte J. T. Dorman, A.S.C. – In affectionate remembrance of our dearest. From his loving wife and little son, Jack'. Another, possibly from his parents, bore the words 'Pte J. T. Dorman – In loving remembrance of our Dear Jack. Lest We Forget'.

John Dorman with his son Jack

By then John's sister Mary, or Molly as she was known, had married his widow's brother, Arthur Hinks, a locomotive fireman. John's widow never remarried. She did clerical work in Rugby and later moved to Hillmorton, where she died. John Dorman lies in Etaples Military Cemetery. It is the largest of the Commonwealth War Graves Commission cemeteries in France. John's grave, numbered III G 20A, is one of more than 11,500 at this hallowed site. His son Jack married in 1939. Jack and his wife Iris had a son Barry, whose second name was John, so keeping the name alive.

M. HAMPSON

A S a professional soldier Mark Hampson had served for more than eighteen years when the Great War started. He was killed in action only three months later. Although it is unlikely that he ever had the opportunity to visit North Kilworth, it was only right that his sacrifice should be honoured on the village's memorial because he had married into a Kilworth family and his widow returned to the village and raised the couple's children there.

Mark Hampson was born on 19 December 1876 in an area of mills and working-class homes near the centre of Manchester. He was not yet two when his millwright father Paul died. His mother Mary took menial work to bring up her family, including the daughter Ann she was expecting when she was widowed. Mark's mother had also died by the time he joined the militia at eighteen, giving the name Mark Harvey for reasons now obscure. Military life obviously suited the dark-haired youngster because after a few months he signed on for the regular army. Persisting with his pseudonym, he enlisted as Private 5019 in the Loyal North Lancashire Regiment on 4 January 1896, committing himself to seven years with the colours and a further five years with the reserve. He was posted to the 2nd Battalion, which had recently returned to its Preston barracks after duty in Ireland. In 1897 the battalion moved to Aldershot and on 22 June that year Hampson and his comrades were sent to London to take part in Queen Victoria's Diamond Jubilee celebrations. He became an unpaid lance corporal the following year before the battalion moved to Dover. On 20 September 1899 Hampson, newly promoted corporal, faced his first foreign posting when the battalion was sent by train to Southampton to embark for Malta on the SS Jelunga.

The Loyals had been at Pembroke Camp on the island only days when the war in South Africa started. However, the 2nd Battalion remained on Malta, although it did send men to the 1st Battalion, which was fighting the Boers, and it also trained mounted infantry for service on the veldt. In February 1901 Hampson was with the depleted battalion when it went to Crete, from where it moved again, to Gibraltar, in May 1902. That September the soldier still known as Harvey decided to end the subterfuge about his identity and made a sworn declaration that he was actually Mark Hampson. The admission did no harm to his army prospects for the following year he was told he could extend his service to twelve years with the colours. By then Hampson was active in the Freemasons, who welcomed many military men into their lodges; Kitchener himself was prominent in the craft. The war in South Africa had been over for almost two years when, on 11 April 1904, Hampson's battalion sailed from Gibraltar for Cape Town en route to Pretoria where it settled into barracks by early May. Hampson was promoted sergeant that September. It was in South Africa that he met Annie Neale who, it is believed, had moved there with a doctor and his family for whom she was a cook. Annie was born in the small south Leicestershire village of Laughton. But her family later moved to North Kilworth where her father Henry was a shepherd on a farm off Station Road. Henry and his wife Elizabeth had another two daughters and a son younger than Annie.

On 31 October 1905 Hampson, by then aged twenty-eight, married Annie, nearly twenty-five, at All Saints, the Anglican church at Booysen, Johannesburg, where the bride lived. A few days before the ceremony Hampson had won permission to go on to complete twenty-one years' service. The couple's first child Eva was born at Pretoria on 4 September 1906. Mother and daughter were among thirty-seven wives and seventy-nine children who embarked with the battalion at Durban on 19 October 1907 for its new posting to Mauritius. The Hampsons' first son Arthur Henry was born there on 28 December 1908. Hampson won his last promotion, to colour sergeant, in January 1909. The battalion's fairly uneventful stay in Mauritius ended that November when it sailed for Bombay from where it went by rail to Poona. Mark and Annie's second son Ronald was born there on 26 October 1910 but was to survive only nine months. He suffered convulsions and died in the family's married quarters at Ghorpuri, Poona, on 9 August 1911.

Hampson had to mask his grief to prepare for important regimental duties later that year. The newly crowned George V had decided to visit India for a great Durbar, an elaborate celebration and confirmation of his position as King Emperor. Mark played a key role when the battalion provided a hundred-strong guard of honour for the King and Queen Mary as they disembarked at Bombay on 3 December from the new P & O ship Medina, which had been fitted out as a royal yacht. The King congratulated the Loyals on their smart appearance. The battalion was involved in more royal escort duties before returning to Poona on 13 January 1912 and Hampson was among nine officers and other ranks awarded a special Durbar Medal for their efforts.

Colour Sergeant Mark Hampson with children Arthur and Eva

A second daughter Ethel Elizabeth, known as Betty, was born to the Hampsons at Poona on 16 February 1913. Servants were relatively cheap to employ, even on an NCO's pay, and Mark and Annie had an *ayah* (nurse or maid) called Rahaby to help look after the *baba log* (children). In the November the Loyals left Poona for Bangalore, where they remained at Baird Barracks until the Great War the following August. Many of the fifty-two British infantry battalions serving in India were recalled to be replaced, in part, by Territorial Force troops. Some battalions went direct to France with the Indian Army Corps while others sailed for England to join divisions still being organised there. The 2nd Battalion Loyal North Lancs was destined for another theatre of war – German East Africa.

Those officers on leave in India were recalled by telegram, each man had a medical inspection – Hampson was passed fit on 30 September 1914 – vets checked the horses and mules, and all equipment, stores and arms necessary

Arthur, Betty on the knee of Rahaby, and Eva in India

for active service in the field were issued. Mark wrote a soldier's will, witnessed by two comrades, leaving all his estate to Annie.

The British planned to send an expeditionary force, comprising nearly eight thousand troops from Indian and British units based in India, to invade and help conquer German East Africa (now Tanzania). Deutsch-Ostafrika, Germany's largest colony, was a tropical expanse of little economic worth. But the aim was to ensure the security of British East Africa (Kenya), which bordered it to the north, and prevent Germany using its colony's ports as havens for warships intent on attacking shipping in sea lanes vital to Britain. The Loyals, with the Indian 101st Grenadiers and two other Indian battalions, were incorporated into the newly-formed 27th (Bangalore) Infantry Brigade, part of the expeditionary force that was to take the town of Tanga. Only forty miles south of the British border, Tanga was the colony's second port, after Dar-es-Salaam, and a railway terminus. The landings would be a costly failure due to muddled planning, little urgency in execution, woeful co-operation betwcen naval and land forces, lack of artillery support and a resourceful and determined German commander.

The battalion's 832 troops sailed from Bombay on 16 October in the troopship Karmala and put into Kilindini harbour on the south side of Mombasa Island on the 31st. The Karmala, eleven other troopships, the light cruiser HMS Fox and three tugs rendezvoused fifteen miles

Sergeant Hampson in early 1900s

off Tanga at dawn on 2 November. The battleship HMS Goliath, which should have provided more Royal Navy support, had to stay at Mombasa with engine problems. The force had so little artillery that small naval guns were hastily rigged with carriages.

The Germans were not expected to oppose the landings. HMS Fox sailed into Tanga harbour to announce an end to an unofficial truce that had been in force between the German authorities and British naval forces. The Germans prevaricated over demands for their unconditional surrender and, because the British did not know if the harbour was mined, it was decided that the landings should be made on a headland one and a half miles east of Tanga town. Tanga was protected by about seventy-five barely trained and inadequately armed men who faced an invasion force many times their number. But several hours were lost before the convoy could be marshalled and the first Indian troops start to wade ashore in an area of mangrove swamps.

The slow build-up of the operation was a gift to Lieutenant Colonel Paul von Lettow-Vorbeck, the German commander, who had anticipated an invasion. His Schutztruppe – local troops under German officers – were deployed in such a way that hard marching or a train ride would soon have them converging on Tanga. They started to arrive in increasing numbers. As the Indian troops moved inland they met firm opposition. At 8am on 3 November there was an urgent call for reinforcements and the Loyals, not scheduled to go ashore until the following day, climbed into lighters which were towed by tugs towards a landing place in pouring rain. The lighters grounded fifty yards from the shore and shallow-draught boats from HMS Fox were used to make a kind of bridge towards the beach. The shirt-sleeved troops had to splash through the last few yards of water. The battalion was ashore by noon and started to dig trenches ready to cover the disembarkation of further troops.

On 4 November the main thrust on Tanga started, with the Loyals in line with Indian troops. It was intensely hot. A steamy rubber plantation and dense sisal facing the battalion made it difficult for everyone to keep in touch and progress was slow. For the first half mile there was no enemy opposition. But vast swarms of wild bees attacked and many soldiers were severely stung on their faces and bare arms and knees.

The Loyals came under intense fire as they approached a steep-sided railway cutting that skirted the town. Their advance lay through tall crops that made it difficult to pinpoint the enemy positions. The Germans' local Ascari troops were shooting at them from a position ahead, others were firing from railway workshops to the left and snipers were hidden in houses in the town. Under the cover of Maxim-guns, the Loyals dashed with bayonets fixed across the cutting then over open ground to the edge of the town, sustaining casualties on the way. The Lancashire men faced machine-gun and rifle fire as they forced their way through streets of hastily barricaded buildings into Tanga. At about 4.30pm the German forces launched a counter-attack, mainly directed against the 101st Grenadiers, who suffered heavy casualties. The Loyals risked being cut off as the enemy got round behind them so they withdrew over the open ground and railway cutting, suffering many casualties from machine-gun fire.

By 5.30pm new positions were firmly established but there was no water in the area. By 11.30pm, after thirteen hours of hard marching and fighting, the Loyals reached the trenches from which they had started that morning. Despite exhaustion and lack of food they worked until 2.30am improving the trenches. It was decided that the whole force should re-embark next day, 5 November. There was to be no taking of Tanga.

The Loyals were the last off the beaches. The muddy nature of the foreshore made it impossible to carry off bulky loads and considerable quantities of ammunition and stores, including wines from the officers' mess, were left behind. On 7 November the Karmala landed the Loyals at Kilindini. After a night in the Customs shed most of the battalion were put on a train to Nairobi and there the Loyals marched into camp on the old parade ground of the King's African Rifles. Mark Hampson was not among them. He was one of 115 casualties the Battalion had suffered out of a total loss for the expeditionary force of 817 killed, missing and wounded. At what point in the operation he died is not recorded.

At some stage the families of the North Lancs' soldiers sailed home from India. Annie Hampson first went to the regiment's home town of Preston but by 1916 she had returned to North Kilworth with her children to be with her parents. After the war ended she was living in Green Lane but later moved to Back Street. She had been awarded a weekly War Office pension of twenty-two shillings (£1.10) in 1915 and in March of that year the Royal Patriotic Fund Corporation granted her £8. Evidently a soldier's widow was not to be trusted with such a princely lump sum and the cash was sent to the Rector's daughter Ursula Cox to be paid 'by small weekly instalments'. The regimental Freemasons also provided assistance. Annie received her husband's medal for long service and good conduct in 1918. Despite being in action so early in the war, Mark did not earn a 1914 Star campaign medal. This was awarded only for service in land operations on the Western Front and he therefore qualified only for the much more common 1914-15 Star.

In 1919 the Hampsons' daughter Eva, by then a twelve-year-old pupil at Kilworth school, passed a scholarship to attend Lutterworth Grammar and cycled there daily. Her sister Betty was to follow suit. In 1922 their brother

Arthur, then thirteen, became the last pupil at Kilworth to leave school on the basis of a labour certificate. From then on every child had to remain until age fourteen. Eva went on to college and became a teacher, Betty worked at the BTH/AEI company in Rugby, Arthur joined the Royal Navy and later the police. Their father would have been proud. Mark Hampson lies in Tanga Memorial Cemetery. Of North Kilworth's fallen he is the farthest from home. His beloved Annie died in 1966 after almost fifty-two years of widowhood.

P. A. KENNA

TO find a military hero of the kind so admired by the Victorians look no further than Paul Kenna. In 1898 this dashing cavalry captain held off a horde of Dervish warriors to pluck to safety a fellow officer whose horse had been shot from under him, then joined in a courageous attempt to recover the body of another comrade. It was the stuff of boys' adventure books. Hollywood might prefer its heroes with more height and hair – Kenna was under 5ft 6in and balding – but here was the real thing: winner of the Victoria Cross, consummate soldier, superb rider, fine judge of bloodstock and, underlying it all, a story of triumph over personal tragedy. The Great War did not allow Kenna a cavalryman's death – he was shot by a sniper amid the trenches of Gallipoli – but North Kilworth, his home for the last few years of his life, was proud to honour his sacrifice.

Paul Aloysius Kenna was born to Irish parents in a smart suburb of Liverpool on 16 August 1862. He was eleven and attending a local Jesuit school when his father James died suddenly. James, a broker, left his widow Julia reasonably well off. She moved to Ramsgate, Kent, where Paul started at St Augustine's Abbey School, run by the Benedictines. He was a hard-working and devout pupil and highly competitive at sports. At age seventeen he moved to Stoneyhurst College, the Roman Catholic public school in Lancashire. Paul's interests included ornithology but he was set on a military career and started cultivating a mighty moustache of the type then favoured by army officers. After he left school in 1881 he went to stay with an uncle in County Durham and was commissioned in a militia battalion of the Durham Light Infantry. When he was twenty-three he went to Sandhurst, where he won prizes for riding and athletics before being commissioned as a second lieutenant in the 2nd Battalion West India Regiment. Kenna served in Jamaica and Sierra Leone then transferred to the more fashionable 21st Hussars in Bangalore, India, in January 1889. He was in the regiment's polo team and took an enthusiastic part in other pastimes of the cavalryman such as pig-sticking, racing, steeple-chasing and hunting, with jackals taking the place of foxes. By the time the Hussars moved to Secunderabad in November 1891 Lieutenant Kenna was building a reputation as one of the army's finest riders whose advice on choosing mounts was keenly sought by other officers. He topped the list of Gentleman Riders in India in 1893, 1894 and 1895.

In 1894 Kenna was introduced to Lady Cecil Bertie, twenty-one-year-old daughter of the Earl of Abingdon. There was an eleven-year age gap but the couple fell in love and were married at St Mary's Catholic Church in the hill station of Ootacamund on 18 July 1895. The previous month, while on leave in Ireland visiting relatives, Kenna had a strange opportunity to demonstrate his bravery. He was walking along the Liffey embankment in Dublin when he saw a man throw himself into the fast-flowing river. He jumped in and held on to the man while a policeman threw down a life buoy. When Kenna retrieved the jacket he had removed before the rescue he found his purse and watch had been stolen. A Royal Humane Society testimonial certificate was some recompense.

Kenna, by now promoted captain, and his bride had only three months of happiness together. Lady Cecil contracted typhoid and died on 3 October. Kenna fell into a deep depression and told a brother officer he wished only for an honourable death in battle. Fellow Hussars were also anxious for action, though for other reasons. India had provided no chance for the 21st to prove itself against an enemy and other cavalry regiments were suggesting its motto should be Thou Shalt Not Kill. Events were to change that.

In March 1896 General Kitchener was told to lead an Anglo-Egyptian invasion of the Sudan, Egypt's southern neighbour. Popularly, it was taken as a move to avenge the death of General Gordon, butchered by followers of the Mahdi in besieged Khartoum in 1885. The Government, however, was chiefly intent on taking over the Sudan before the French could. After the Mahdi, or Islamic 'expected one', died the Khalifa, or 'deputy', took over leadership of the Mahdists, known as Dervishes. Kitchener's force was to make a thousand-mile push up the Nile from Cairo to take Khartoum and the

Khalifa's new, nearby capital of Omdurman. By September 1896 Kitchener's force had taken Dongola two hundred miles south of the Egyptian border. The next month the 21st Hussars left India for Egypt and settled into barracks near Cairo. Early in 1897 the khaki-clad regiment started desert training. The regiment learnt in the April that, for administrative reasons, it was to become the 21st Lancers. Nine-foot lances were issued for the men and drills with the unfamiliar weapon started. Meanwhile Kitchener continued his advance and in July 1898 the 21st was sent to join his force. B Squadron, with Kenna as second-in-command under Major J. Fowle, was the first to leave Cairo by rail. On 2 September Kenna and his comrades were with the rest of the Anglo-Egyptian force outside Omdurman, with its flat-roofed mud houses dominated by the dome of the Mahdi's tomb. Kitchener's 25,800 men were encamped on the banks of the Nile in a zariba, an enclosure protected by thorn bushes and a trench.

About forty-one thousand Dervish warriors, most of them clad in the jibbah, a loose white cotton tunic with coloured patches, attacked. Swords, spears and old Remington rifles were no match for Kitchener's gunboats, artillery, rapid-firing Maxim guns and Lee-Metford magazine rifles. The Dervishes lost an estimated two thousand dead and four thousand wounded. Not one Dervish penetrated the zariba. There were fewer than sixty British and Egyptian casualties. Kitchener was anxious to get his infantry into Omdurman before the Khalifa's remaining warriors could reach the town and make a stand. The 21st Lancers' moment had come.

It was still only 7.30am when Kitchener sent the regiment on reconnaissance to see if any Dervishes might threaten the infantry's advance. 'Head them off if possible from Omdurman,' was the order received by the Lancers' commanding officer Lieutenant Colonel R. H. Martin. As the regiment rode towards Omdurman it was confronted by two hundred Dervishes of the Hadendoa tribe, dubbed Fuzzy Wuzzies by Tommies because of their frizzed and stiffened hair. The warriors, only thirty-one of them armed with rifles, were standing in line on a slight ridge. Martin estimated there might be a total of a thousand Dervishes in the vicinity but was confident that his force of thirty-four officers, 412 men plus a correspondent from *The Times* could deal with them. One of Martin's officers was a young lieutenant of the 4th Hussars who had wangled an attachment to the 21st. His name was Winston Churchill. The four squadrons lined up to face the enemy at three hundred

Paul Kenna VC, hero of the famed cavalry charge at Omdurman

yards' range. Martin did not know that a khor, or dry water bed, of which the ridge was the nearest edge, concealed 2,600 Dervishes.

The bugler sounded Trot but the cavalry picked up pace so rapidly that further orders of Canter, Gallop and Charge were never sounded. Kenna was the only officer to wield a lance; the others held their swords pointing forward at the enemy. With less than a hundred yards to go the 21st discovered it was riding into a trap. The Dervishes were twelve deep in the khor, twenty deep in places, but every rider was committed. Thirty seconds after starting its charge the 21st hurtled into the khor at twenty miles per hour. While horses were in mid-air the Dervishes thrust spears into their bellies or slashed their hamstrings with knives and swords. The warriors hacked at the head of any rider thrown from his disabled animal. Major W. G. Crole-Wyndham, the regiment's second-in-command, landed well but a Dervish shot his horse. The animal pressed on for a few yards before falling. Crole-Wyndham landed on his feet and, with his Mauser pistol in one hand and sword in the other, slashed and fired at Dervishes closing in for the kill. Kenna, with B Squadron in the centre of the line, had entered the khor where it was widest and most densely packed. But his grey charger Rainbow landed well and Kenna saw the unhorsed major. He pulled Crole-Wyndham up behind him and both officers fired their pistols into the mass of warriors. Kenna spurred on Rainbow and gained a few crucial yards before the horse threw them. Crole-Wyndham fought his way to the far side of the khor and Kenna managed to remount and get through. Kenna's B Squadron comrade and close friend Lieutenant René de Montmorency had come out of the khor when he saw Crole-Wyndham with a spear-wielding Dervish horseman in pursuit. De Montmorency rode at the warrior and shot him. He then came across the body of another B Squadron officer, Lieutenant Robert Grenfell, who had been pitched from his horse and hacked to death. Intent on preventing further mutilation of the corpse, de Montmorency called to Kenna and Corporal Swarbrick. Those two remained in the saddle to ward off the enemy as de Montmorency dismounted and struggled to lift the body on to his horse. The terrified animal bolted and Kenna and Swarbrick rode to bring it back while de Montmorency, armed only with a revolver, stood guard over his fallen comrade. The three men tried again to recover the body but, with Dervishes closing in, they had to ride off to join other members of the regiment, who had chopped and battered their way through and come into line 150 yards beyond the khor. Many were ready to charge back through the Dervishes but Martin quickly assessed that the likely cost would be too great. Instead he led his men to face the khor at right angles to the line of charge. Two squadrons dismounted and opened fire with their carbines. The Dervishes advanced but the Lancers' accurate shooting pushed them slowly back. The bodies of Grenfell, the only officer to die, and twenty men were recovered for burial. The number of Dervish dead numbered perhaps seventy. The Lancers, having made the last full regimental cavalry charge of the British Army, set off to return to Cairo on 6 September.

Kenna and de Montmorency were awarded the Victoria Cross, as was Private Thomas Byrne, also of B Squadron, who had fought on after being shot through his sword arm. The three were invested with the VC by Queen Victoria at Osborne, her Isle of Wight home, on 6 January 1899. She had by then approved the 21st Lancers assuming the title Empress of India's Regiment. The Grenfell family presented Kenna and de Montmorency with silver cups, each engraved with the words In Recognition of a Gallant Deed. Crole-Wyndham recovered a hoof from his dead horse and had it mounted as an inkstand for Kenna.

Far from finding death in battle, Kenna had emerged from beneath his pall of grief with renewed spirit. In October of 1899, as the Boer War started, he sailed to South Africa as Assistant Provost Marshal to the Cavalry Division on the staff of General French. Kenna was appointed brigade major in 1900 and the following year was given command of a column. He was involved in the Relief of Kimberley and several other operations including those at Colesburg, Paardeberg and Zand River. When the war ended on 31 May 1902 he had been awarded a DSO and gained two mentions in dispatches. He was promoted substantive major on 7 September of that year and two months later was selected for special service in Somaliland (now Somalia). He was appointed Commandant of the Mounted Troops of the Somaliland Field Force and was involved in two expeditions against the Mad Mullah, a religious leader who had been raiding friendly tribes. In December 1903 Kenna led a reconnaissance force to determine the strength of the enemy encamped at Jidballi. At daybreak on the 19th Kenna sent in the British Mounted Infantry, who engaged the enemy for five hours. On 9 January 1904 a general advance against the Mullah began. The British repulsed three desperate charges by six to eight thousand Somali riflemen and spearmen. Kenna's mounted troops chased the enemy for twelve miles, galloping close, dismounting, firing, then renewing the pursuit until Kenna finally called them off. The Mullah was hounded into Italian territory and his followers' morale was broken. Kenna, praised for his dash and energy, was mentioned in dispatches three times, rewarded with the brevet rank of lieutenant colonel and returned to his regiment in England in June 1904 with his reputation further enhanced.

Soon afterwards he attended a house party where he met Angela Mary Hibbert, daughter of a Catholic family. They married at the Brompton Oratory in London on 2 March 1905 when Kenna was forty-two and his bride twenty-six. The Kennas were to have two daughters, born in 1906 and 1909. On 7 September 1906 Kenna took over command of the 21st Lancers and on 1 December was promoted brevet colonel and appointed ADC to Edward VII. His tenure with the Lancers ended in September 1910 when he became a substantive colonel and went on half pay. On 1 April 1912 his appointment to command the Notts and Derby Mounted Brigade, Northern Command, was announced.

During his England-based years Kenna played polo, rode hundreds of winners on the flat and in cross-country and cemented his reputation as a showjumper. In November 1910 he led the British team at the New York International Horse Show where he came second on Deliberation in the heavy chargers class. Kenna also led the British equestrian team at the 1912 Stockholm Olympics where it performed poorly, partly through lack of time for preparation. His greatest triumph came at the Royal Naval and Military Tournament at Olympia in 1913. Riding Harmony, he won the King's Cup, which George V presented to him.

In 1911 Kenna and his family were living in fashionable Sloane Street in Knightsbridge but soon after moved to Kilworth Hall. Mrs Kenna's family once lived at Bilton Grange, on the other side of Rugby. His North Kilworth base gave Kenna opportunity to ride with the Pytchley Hunt, which often had distinguished former military men in the field. Guy Paget, chronicler of Pytchley lore, remembered Kenna as 'a great little rider, gassing away merrily'. One old friend of Kenna was to recall, 'He had many a toss, chasing, hunting and playing polo, but there was never anyone who took them more cheerily.' Kenna took horses to the goods yard at Welford and Kilworth station where the sudden blast of steam from locomotives helped test his mounts' steadiness.

He attended services at the Catholic church in the grounds of Bosworth Hall and supported such Kilworth events as the flower show when duty permitted. He was taking part in a riding exhibition in Vichy in June 1914 when worries of impending war meant he had to dash home to his command. His horses Deliberation and Harmony were left behind and requisitioned by the French army. Kenna's brigade, comprising the South Notts Yeomanry, Sherwood Yeomanry and Derbyshire Yeomanry, was one of four brigades of the 2nd Mounted Division. Kenna, now promoted brigadier general, went to Egypt with the division in April 1915. It was intended for mounted service in Turkey once Gallipoli had been occupied. But the invasion there stalled and, with casualties mounting, it was decided that the division would be of more use as infantry. Kenna's brigade left its horses with a skeleton staff at Giza and embarked from Alexandria on 14 August. The division landed unscathed at Suvla Bay from where it was to take part in attacks to take key hills inland. In a temporary reshuffle of commands Kenna was put in charge of 2nd Mounted Division. On 21 August the division came under heavy Turkish fire as it crossed a dry salt lake before being sent immediately to storm the heights. With the enemy well entrenched and daylight failing, the attack was halted with heavy casualties.

Nevertheless Kenna was considered to have organised the attempt well and conducted the retirement satisfactorily. In the next few days he went back to his 3rd (Notts and Derby) Brigade, which became occupied digging a new trench to straighten out a section of the front line. On the night of 29 August Kenna went forward with his young ADC Lord Hartington and Captain Hamilton Delmege to inspect the work. A communication trench had not been completed so the officers had to cross thirty yards of open ground. They had only five yards to go when, at 9.30pm, a Turkish sniper fired. The bullet smashed Kenna's elbow before entering his body. Stretcher bearers managed to carry the mortally wounded officer to a field hospital. Two priests visited him at different times in the large tent where he lay and the last rites were performed. Kenna died in the early hours of Monday 30 August and was buried later that day. His body was later re-interred in Lala Baba Cemetery which faces over Suvla Bay. The cemetery contains the graves of two hundred soldiers from the UK. Kenna's, numbered II A 1, bears the epitaph On Whose Soul Sweet Jesus Have Mercy. May He Rest In Peace. Aged fifty-three, Kenna was the oldest of North Kilworth's fallen. His widow left the village and remarried in 1919.

M. E. LLOYD

ETON is a name seen by many as synonymous with privilege. In the Great War one 'privilege' for many former pupils of the most famous of public schools was the right to sacrifice their lives for their country. Old Etonians who served in 1914-18 numbered 5,650, of whom 1,157 died. That is more than one in five; poor odds indeed. Among those killed was Meyricke Entwisle Lloyd, eldest son of Henry Lloyd, a JP and gentleman of independent means, whose own father Richard was a banker. Henry had an estate at Dolobran in Montgomeryshire, where he had served as a captain in the county's Yeomanry. In 1878 he married Caroline Entwisle, sister of John Entwisle, at North Kilworth, so explaining Meyricke's second name. It is likely that Caroline had been staying with her brother at Kilworth House. The Entwisles, as has been noted, were a Lancashire land-owning family. Their wealth was based on the cotton trade.

Meyricke was born at The Crescent, Scarborough, possibly a regular seaside retreat for the Lloyds, on 31 May 1880. The couple already had a daughter Gwladys. Meyricke was followed by another sister Nesta and brother Stanley. In the 1880s Henry Lloyd took Pitsford Hall, Northamptonshire, and neighbouring land. He kept his Welsh property but the 18th century hall became the family home where a governess and six servants were employed. Pitsford was some fifteen miles from North Kilworth so it is reasonable to assume that the Lloyd children were taken to visit their uncle there from time to time. The four were still in their teens when their mother died at Pitsford in 1896 at the age of forty-seven. By then Meyricke had been at Eton College, in Mr Austen Leigh's house, for about two years. He left Eton in July 1896, having made no great impact academically. Three months later his father married again. Henry's bride Mary Vere Gosling was aged thirty-nine. She had a son Cecil Henry the following year but this half-brother to Meyricke survived only twenty-four hours. Meyricke's father died in January 1902, aged sixty-one, and it appears that his daughters went to live with their Uncle John at Kilworth House. (John Bertie Norreys Entwisle had married Mary Dalton, niece of Lady Lisgar, in 1881, but the couple had no children of their own.)

Meyricke was already in the army at the time of his father's death. His visits to Kilworth were therefore probably less frequent than previously but

M. E. Lloyd (second row down, sixth from right) at Eton in 1895

John Entwisle maintained his interest in the welfare of his sister's son, who shared his enthusiasm for hunting. Meyricke had joined the 3rd (Militia) Battalion of the Northamptonshire Regiment in May 1899. He was a second lieutenant in A Company when, in January 1900, the battalion marched through Northampton, bands playing, to board special trains at Castle Station on the way to take up garrison duties in Aldershot. The move was prompted by the demands of the war in South Africa. However the battalion was not called abroad and moved to Portland in the March.

In June 1900 Lloyd, fair-haired and 5ft 8in, was granted a regular commission as a second lieutenant in the Royal Welch Fusiliers. Details of his early service are sketchy but in 1901 he was with the regiment's 2nd Battalion in Peking where the Boxer Rebellion, an uprising against foreign legations, had been put down. He was on home leave in August 1902 when he joined his sisters at North Kilworth flower show. He later served in India, where he showed a talent for polo, and was promoted lieutenant and, in 1911, captain.

Lloyd was thirty-two and based at barracks in Dublin when, on 1 October 1912, he married Elizabeth Ramsay, twenty-five-year-old daughter of Brigadier General William Alexander Ramsay, at Cheltenham. Pitsford's Rector John White travelled to Gloucestershire to perform the ceremony. Ten of Lloyd's friends from the 2nd Battalion marked the occasion by presenting him with a silver plate with their signatures engraved on it. The newlyweds were already remotely related. A great-aunt of Meyricke on the Entwisle side had married Elizabeth's great-uncle Sir Alexander Ramsay (3rd Baronet), sometime MP for Rochdale. Lloyd and his wife made their home at Trewythen, Gresford, three miles from Wrexham, where the Royal Welch had their depot, and in the Wynnstay hunt country favoured by the regiment's officers. The Lloyds' daughter Mary Doreen was born on 21 July 1913.

At the outbreak of war a little over a year later Lloyd was in the 3rd (Reserve) Battlion but was transferred to the 1st Battalion, which was in camp at Lyndhurst, Hampshire, having been brought back from Malta. It was about to be sent to Flanders as part of 22nd Brigade 7th Division. The Royal Welch Fusiliers included among its wartime officers two of the conflict's great poets: Siegfried Sassoon, who also wrote *Memoirs of an Infantry Officer,* and Robert Graves, author of *Goodbye to All That*. (During the war the regiment was correctly termed the Royal Welsh Fusiliers but the name was officially restored to the previously preferred Welch in 1920).

Lloyd and the rest of the 1st Battalion left Lyndhurst on 4 October 1914 and boarded the Leyland liner Winifredian at nearby Southampton early the next day. After delays and diversions the battalion disembarked at Zeebrugge on the 7th and was taken by rail to billets four miles south of Bruges. The Royal Welch then took another train to Ghent and for the next few days put in some long marches as they were moved from point to point in response to reports of enemy movements. But there was little contact with the Germans. On the 14th the battalion marched into Ypres, exhausted from lack of food and sleep. Two days later the division moved out in three columns to establish a line to the east and south-east of the town. The Royal Welch, as advance guard, entered the village of Zonnebeke to learn that a patrol of Uhlans (German cavalry) had left twenty minutes before. The battalion, with the rest of 22nd Brigade, moved to Becelaere on the 18th. The real action was about to begin in what would become known as the First Battle of Ypres.

Polo chums M. E. Lloyd (far left) and E. R. Kearsley (far right)

On the 19th the whole division was ordered to advance against firmly dug-in German forces. Lloyd's battalion, with the 2nd Warwickshires, had as its objective the village of Kleythoek where the Germans had fortified advance posts. Despite lack of artillery support, the battalion rapidly pressed home its attack. It was within two hundred yards of its objective when the division was ordered to withdraw because large numbers of German reinforcements had appeared. At this point practically the whole battalion was fighting the enemy at close range and there were considerable casualties. Luckily the Germans did not pursue the retiring troops too closely and the battered battalion was back in trenches in Zonnebeke by dusk.

Next day the enemy guns started hammering the British positions. Then, on the 21st, the Germans attacked at daybreak. In some places their line was only a hundred yards from the British trenches. At such close range the enemy artillery was lethally accurate; trenches were pulverised and many casualties

Captain Lloyd (rear, third from left) ready for Belgium in 1914

were caused by shells bursting actually on the parapet. The Royal Welch maintained accurate and rapid rifle fire but were running low on ammunition and both of their machine-guns were out of action. At about 6pm the Germans took part of the line. Soldiers of two companies were taken prisoner because they refused to abandon their trenches even though sections on either side had been destroyed. The Germans did not press their advantage at this stage and the remains of the battalion withdrew in the early hours to a line 250 yards to the rear. Lloyd was not with his men. He was reported killed, one of twenty-three officers and almost seven hundred men lost in three days by the battalion, which would later receive a further mauling in the defence of Ypres.

The precise date of Lloyd's death is uncertain. The regimental diary listed him as having been killed on 20 or 21 October but word was later received from the German authorities that, having been shot in the chest, he died while in enemy hands on the 23rd. The Germans buried him at Passchendaele. He was thirty-four.

Lloyd's widow Elizabeth with daughter Mary in 1917 or 1918

His wife of just over two years, left with a daughter not old enough to grow up remembering her father, at least faced no financial hardship. Meyricke, well provided for when his father died, left an estate grossing £25,544. On 8 January 1919 Elizabeth Lloyd married one of her husband's old army friends, Major Edward Reginald Kearsley. It was said that Meyricke had urged his former polo chum to take care of Elizabeth if he were to lose his life. The major was described by a soldier who served under him on the Western Front as 'much respected, a neat precise little man with fair hair'. Another of Kearsley's attributes was courage; he was wounded twice and earned a DSO and Bar by the end of the war. He and Elizabeth lived at Ruabon, on the opposite side of Wrexham from the Lloyds' former home, and had a son Nigel two years after the war. Elizabeth had tried to learn the location of Meyricke's grave but it was the end of 1921 before the Imperial (now Commonwealth) War Graves Commission could offer any information. It led only to years of more uncertainty and distress. The Commission had learned from civilians in Passchendaele that the Germans had moved Meyricke's remains to a cemetery 'in the direction of Gheluwe'. In Gheluwe German military cemetery a large grave said to contain unknown British soldiers was opened in October 1920. The bodies included those of a Royal Welch captain but the only clue to identity was a white or khaki handkerchief with mauve rings. Despite the lack of evidence a cross was erected bearing Meyricke's name and details preceded by the words 'Believed to be'. The Commission wrote to Elizabeth again in 1925 to explain that the British soldiers in Gheluwe cemetery had been re-interred at Harlebeke New British Cemetery. As the Commission could trace no authority for the erection of a cross bearing Meyricke's name it had taken special notes when the remains were removed with a view to securing definite identification. The fallen officer was, however, nearly six feet tall, three inches taller than Meyricke. The Commission also pointed out that Meyricke was not the only officer who could be buried in the grave as other Royal Welch officers who became casualties at the same time were not in named graves.

Elizabeth wrote to say she was unable to accept the description of the remains as referring to Meyricke and the inscription on the cross was amended to read 'Unknown British Officer R. W. Fus: October 1914'. Today Meyricke Lloyd's name is on Panel 22 of the Menin Gate, the huge memorial in Ypres which honours more than fifty-four thousand men with no known grave. In North Kilworth, the Entwisle connection was sufficient to ensure Lloyd's name appeared on the village memorial. John Entwisle, widowed at the end of 1916, married Florence Ramsay in April 1919. Florence had Entwisle as well as Ramsay forebears and was a second cousin of Meyricke's widow. Meyricke's daughter Mary, who lived into her nineties, recalled being taken to visit her Uncle Jack and Aunt Flossie at Kilworth House between the wars.

As a historical aside, Elizabeth Lloyd/Kearsley's brother Admiral Sir Bertram Home Ramsay organised the evacuation of British and Allied troops from Dunkirk in 1940, played a major part in the planning for the invasions of North Africa and Sicily and planned the naval part of the D-Day landings in 1944. John Entwisle died in 1945 and Florence in 1953, after which Kilworth House was sold. The Entwisle home which acted as backdrop to the tragedies of 1914 is now a hotel.

A. SPRIGGS

TWO Spriggs brothers served in the Great War. The elder, James Henry, was wounded but returned home; his brother Albert died soon after being sent to Belgium. They were the sons of James Spriggs senior, who came from Walcote, a village a couple of miles west of North Kilworth, and spent his life in farm work in the area. James senior married Annie Chambers, a baker's daughter from Walcote, in 1873. The couple were living in Welford, where James had a job as a groom, when Albert was born on 13 March 1880. By 1901 James was widowed and working as a farm wagoner at North Kilworth where he lived on the Leicester road with his twenty-three-year-old daughter Annie.

That year's census shows Albert Spriggs serving as a gunner with the Royal Field Artillery but further details have not come to light. However, by 1915 he had become Private 12431 Spriggs in the 2nd Battalion Duke of Wellington's (West Riding Regiment), having enlisted at Keighley in Yorkshire. The battalion arrived in France less than two weeks after the outbreak of war but Spriggs did not cross the Channel until 18 February 1915. A few days later he and fifty-nine other ranks under Lieutenant

Rowland Owen (killed two months later) joined the battalion which, having endured an awful winter, was alternating between billets in Ypres and trenches in nearby Zillebeke. March was relatively uneventful for the battalion but in the early part of the month Spriggs was wounded in circumstances not recorded. He succumbed to his injuries on Monday 8 March, five days short of his thirty-fifth birthday. He was the only soldier of the battalion to die that day. News of Albert's death reached his sister Annie a week later. 'Much sympathy is felt for his aged father,' said the *Rugby Advertiser*. Annie was by then married to Arthur Whyles, who also joined up.

Comrades whom Spriggs had so little time to get to know were among the hundreds of casualties suffered by the battalion in the fierce fighting for Hill 60 near Ypres a few weeks after his death. Albert Spriggs lies in grave IV A 47 in enclosure number two of Bedford House Cemetery outside Ypres. His grieving father died in 1924 aged seventy-five.

G. W. STOCK

THE only uniform that young railwayman George Stock anticipated wearing was that of the London and North Western. However, the country was in greater need of soldiers than station porters and Stock answered the call – only to die as a result of influenza without getting any further than a training camp fewer than fifty miles from home. Such were the cards of fate dealt by the Great War.

The Stocks were a railway family. Signalman William Stock had gone to work in the box at Welford and Kilworth station and lived in Church Street, North Kilworth, with his wife Minnie. The couple hailed from Northamptonshire, he from Bozeat and she from nearby Yardley Hastings. William's brother Joseph also worked for the railway, as a carter, and lived with his wife and children in Kilworth for a while. George, the first child of William and Minnie, was born on 22 February 1897 and christened George William by Rector Belgrave that May. His brother Harry, born the following year, would become a signalman like the boys' father. The lads had younger sisters Sylvia, Margaret and Evelyn.

George Stock was to swap railway uniform for that of a soldier

George attended the village school and at Sunday school in 1907 he gained top marks in his class for attendance and conduct. That year he was also chosen as king to partner the schoolchildren's May queen Edith Stapleton. His guards were Willie Clarke and Will Burbidge, both of whom would serve in the war. Edith was sister of Alf Stapleton, another future soldier. George was fond of drawing and colouring and some of his pictures of, for instance, flowers and a country house have survived.

In July 1909 he received his labour certificate to leave school at the same time as Billy Pebody and Will Cheney. What work he took while waiting to follow his father into railway employment is not recalled but eventually he was taken on as a porter. Photos of him out of his railway uniform show an immaculately dressed young man proudly displaying on his lapel the badge of the National Union of Railwaymen. George was a slender youth, nearly 5ft 11in tall while weighing under ten stones, but that did not prevent him performing his work duties diligently. Conscription had recently been introduced when, on 15

G. Stock wearing union badge

February 1916, a week short of his nineteenth birthday, George attested at Market Harborough. He was not summoned for duty immediately but was put on the reserve and continued working at stations including Welford and Kilworth and Bridge Street in Northampton. He was called for an army medical that December and joined the 2nd Training Reserve Battalion of the Leicestershire Regiment at its Glen Parva depot on 15 January 1917. Private Stock's records show two regimental numbers, 36790 and TR/5/4960.

Within days he was sent to Rugeley Camp on the heathland of Cannock Chase in Staffordshire. The weather was bitterly cold but George was determined to make the most of his new life. On 21 January he sent his mother a postcard, telling her he was preparing to be vaccinated and that he was off to spend a relaxing hour at the YMCA. The card, with its green halfpenny stamp, had printed on the front a sentimental picture typical of the era. A soldier is penning a message home and, inset, is a picture of the patiently waiting wife or sweetheart. Another card sent by George had a comic verse which, although titled Rugeley Camp, appeared with minor variations elsewhere, satirising the rigours of life in various military establishments. A couple of typical lines ran, 'Inside the huts there's rats as big as any nanny goat. Last night a soldier saw one trying on his overcoat'. The verse ends with the catchphrase 'But we're not downhearted yet'. On the rear of the card George pencilled his message, 'All being well I shall try and get my photo taken shortly in the camp. The other side isn't very far wrong but I haven't yet come across a rat. Au revoir.'

Camps such as Rugeley, with hundreds of men thrust together, were inevitably prone to infections. In February George was taken into the camp's hospital with influenza. His temperature soared to 102 degrees, subsided then peaked at 103 before returning to normal again. His head and body were racked with pain. When complications set in George's parents were called to his bedside and were with him when he died at 2.30pm on Friday 16 February 1917. George's brief army service was enough for him to be honoured by a military funeral, conducted at North Kilworth by Rector Cox on 21 February. His coffin, returned to the village under the charge of a sergeant, was draped with the Union Flag as it was borne into church by four soldiers. The large congregation watched as three volleys were fired at the graveside and a bugler sounded *Last Post*. The wreaths included one from the teachers and pupils at the school. It was the eve of George's twentieth birthday. Local newspaper obituaries told how, in civilian life, he 'had won for himself the character of thorough attention to, and trustworthiness in, his duties' and presented 'a bright example of duty done bravely and quietly'.

Family life, of course, went on, and when Kilworth's schoolchildren danced around the May Pole in 1918 it was George's thirteen-year-old sister Maggie who was queen. After the war the Stocks at least had the consolation of the safe return of their other son Harry from army service. And, unlike so many other families who would never be able to visit the graves of sons in France or farther afield, they could glean some comfort from knowing George lay in the churchyard half a minute from their front door. The memorial plaque and scroll marking his death were cherished by his parents for the rest of their lives. William Stock continued working at Welford and Kilworth station for many years. Surely, in quieter moments in the signal box high above the tracks, his thoughts turned to the son whose own railway career was cut so tragically short.

S. W. WICKES

THE youngest of North Kilworth's sons to die in the Great War was Sydney Wickes, nineteen years and five months old when he lost his life on the Western Front in 1918. He was the grandson of widowed Elizabeth Wickes, who ran the bakery near The Green where some villagers would pay a penny to have their Sunday joints cooked in her ovens while they were at church or in the pub. She was helped in the business by sons John and William while their brothers Tom and Ted worked at Ball's. There was another son George and a daughter Mary Jane (Polly), who worked as a dressmaker. William was Sydney's father. William had decided on a change of job and was working as a house painter in Uppingham, Rutland, where he was living with his wife Jane when Sydney, their first child, was born on 11 October 1898. The parents, who had married the previous year, took the baby back to North Kilworth to be christened Sydney William when he was three weeks old. The family later moved to Nelson Street in Market Harborough where William became a greengrocer. Sydney's younger brothers Cyril and Alec were born in the town.

For some lost reason Sydney spent at least part of his childhood at his grandma's home and was still only three when he started at Kilworth school on 10 April 1902. He matured into a diligent pupil both there and at Sunday school. He recorded the normal absences through childhood illnesses and was off school for a month in 1907 after spraining his knee when he collided with an iron post at playtime. But at the annual school treats in 1907 and 1910 the Rector presented Sydney with a prize for top attendance in his

Sunday school class. Another minor success was his third place in the children's wild flowers section at the annual flower show at Kilworth House in 1909.

It is not known what work Sydney took after leaving school but he was in the army before he was nineteen. He is recorded as having enlisted at Rugby and was initially Private 381081 of the Leicestershire Regiment. In 1917 he was in camp on Cannock Chase, where George Stock died. Soon after his arrival Sydney sent a postcard to his friend, George's brother Harry, saying, 'Haven't heard from you yet. Do you know when you are coming up? Afraid you won't get in our mob. We're full up. We have been isolated for spotted fever and measles but we came out yesterday. Feeling fit now and enjoying myself.'

At some stage Sydney was transferred to the 2/6th South Staffordshire Regiment as Private 42371 and he was with that battalion when, as part of 176th Brigade 59th Division, it was one of the units that faced the German spring offensive in 1918. From 10 March the battalion was in brigade reserve south of Arras. Sydney and his comrades of G Platoon C Company were taking the chance to bathe and generally freshen up although large working parties were sent out at night to repair and wire the defences. The enemy fired high explosive shells near them on several mornings and each dawn Stand To was ordered in case of a German attack. On the morning of 18 March the battalion moved up to the reserve defence line near Ecoust but returned to camp at about 8am. Next day the battalion left camp to relieve the 2/4th Leicesters at Bullecourt about eleven kilometres north-east of Bapaume. All was fairly quiet on the 20th and there were no casualties. It was the calm before the hellish storm. The offensive started the following day. The Germans began heavy shelling of the areas behind the Staffords between 2 and 3am. Then from 4 to 8am the front and support lines were battered with high explosive and gas shells. At 9am the German infantry came over in massed formation and there was no stopping them. They captured the front line and pulled off a flanking move to reach the Staffords' railway reserve and battalion headquarters. The colonel, adjutant, four company commanders and seventeen other officers were reported missing, as were about six hundred other ranks, Wickes among them. From the transport lines fifty bandsmen and other specialists were hastily gathered under a major and went up to hold a portion of the front line of the third system of defence, east of

Mory, until relieved at 4am on the 22nd. But the German advance continued and Wickes's family was told he was presumed killed on the 21st.

He did not live to spend the 3s 6d (17.5p) sent to him from home in an envelope containing a slip with the message 'With best wishes for Easter from the parishioners of North Kilworth'. Sydney Wickes has no known grave but his name is among those honoured in the bay of the Arras Memorial.

* * *

ONE of North Kilworth's war dead is not named on the memorial for the simple reason that he was the enemy. Max Franzke was among the German prisoners of war brought to the village in 1918. About forty of them arrived on 19 February and were held at The Hawthorns to be put to work on the land. Franzke, a farmer before the war, was a private in the 441 Reserve Infantry Regiment when he was captured. He died at the Hawthorns on 31 October 1918 as a result of pneumonia brought on by influenza. He was twenty-six. The German was buried in North Kilworth churchyard, just inside the south wall, on 4 November with the Rector and a Roman Catholic priest from Husbands Bosworth in attendance. A simple wooden cross was erected

German prisoners of war outside the Hawthorns in Kilworth

and the Imperial War Graves Commission arranged for five shillings (25p) a year to be sent to the Rector towards maintaining the grave. In 1936 the Commission wrote to say slate crosses were being sent by the Germans for graves of their soldiers. However, Franzke's cross seems not to have been replaced. Another world war had come and gone when the German and British Governments agreed that German servicemen buried in Britain should be brought together in a new burial ground on Cannock Chase, Staffordshire. Franzke's remains were quietly exhumed in 1961 and reburied in the cemetery which, ironically, is close to the site of the military camp where some of North Kilworth's soldiers of 1914-18 were sent for basic training. Franzke is one of more than 2,140 Germans of the First World War and more than 2,780 of the Second who are buried there. He lies in Grave 38, Row 2, Block 13.

IN THANKFUL APPRECIATION

THIS chapter's heading is taken from the inscription on the memorial that honours those who served and returned home safely. These are their stories.

G. BALL

THE uniform suited him. Joining the Leicestershire Yeomanry also offered young George Ball the company of good pals, trips to camp, a sense of pride in serving his country and the prestige due to any cavalryman. The Yeomanry, mounted arm of the Territorial Force, demanded only part-time commitment. Pre-war recruits such as Ball agreed to undertake basic training and attend a minimum of eight drill sessions a year. They could be called up as part of the reserve in a national emergency but there was no compulsion to serve abroad. When Ball cheerily signed up in 1913 he could not have guessed that he would be among the first men from North Kilworth to be sent to the Western Front or that he would serve until 1919, rising through the ranks to become an officer.

George Ball was born on 15 January 1896, first child of George Ball senior, owner of the implement works in North Kilworth, and his wife Maria. The infant, baptised at St Andrew's on 5 August that year, eventually had four brothers and three sisters *(see V. E. Ball, The Fallen)*. He was a game youngster and when he was six he came second in the fifty-yards race for under-eights at the 1902 flower show sports. George is thought to have attended South Kilworth school for a while before starting classes at North Kilworth in 1905. He later attended Wyggeston boys' school in Leicester. George inherited his father's talent for singing and was in the church choir. When the village's minstrel troupe performed in a concert at the Belgrave Memorial Hall in 1909 the schoolboy's rendition of *Santa Claus is Coming for the Morning* won applause to rival that for George senior's *At a Minute to Seven Last Night*.

Schooling completed, George started learning the craft of a wheelwright in the family business. He was seventeen when, on 6 April 1913, he signed up for four years' service in the Leicestershire Yeomanry (Prince Albert's Own). His workmates Ted Cheney and Walter Morley also joined. George became Private 1944 in D Squadron, which recruited from the Lutterworth area. There was a certain old-time cachet to the Yeomanry but army reforms making it part of the Territorial Force put the emphasis on preparing for modern warfare. George Ball attended annual camp in 1913, taking part in manoeuvres, marches and dismounted actions in the countryside. There was practice with a Maxim gun and instruction in reconnaissance and map-reading. Concerts and riding and shooting competitions provided an element of fun.

At the outbreak of war on 4 August 1914 the Leicestershire Yeomanry mobilised as three squadrons and a regimental headquarters. The men of D Squadron were distributed among the others and George was allocated to the Leicester-based B Squadron. He and a dozen other comrades were seen off at the Great Central station in Lutterworth on the first weekend of the war. The town's band played cheery tunes and local dignitaries were on the platform. The soldiers were in good spirits even though many of their friends were in tears. Cheers were raised as the train steamed out. The destination was Grantham where the regiment formed part of the North Midland Mounted Brigade. By early September the brigade was at Diss in Norfolk. Volunteers prepared to waive their right not to serve overseas were called for and George Ball was among the ninety-four per cent of Leicestershire Yeomanry soldiers who signed the consent form. Those who did not do so were sent back to form the nucleus of a reserve unit. For George and his friends the great adventure was about to start.

The regiment went by train to Southampton and on the night of 2 November boarded ship, arriving at Le Havre next morning. The commanding officer Lieutenant Colonel the Hon Percy Evans-Freke had served in the South African war but many of his men had never been abroad. The regiment took the train to St Omer and was soon in the saddle heading eastwards towards Ypres. At the village of Esquerdes George heard firing in anger for the first time but nothing came of it and the next few days were uneventful.

George Ball, as an officer cadet, with his bride Elsie in 1918

Then, on a night of rain, hail and wind, the regiment rode into Ypres as shells fell amid ruined and blazing houses. The Yeomen, tired from their long ride through the Flanders mud, made camp with shells continuing to whistle overhead. Next day they sought refuge in a nearby wood. That night the regiment left its horses behind and went forward into the reserve trenches. With daylight came renewed heavy shelling. It was 9pm before the regiment was relieved and the soldiers filed away over the freezing ground with bullets whizzing over their heads.

The Leicestershire Yeomanry, now part of the 7th Cavalry Brigade, had just emerged from the First Battle of Ypres, having tasted real soldiering while suffering only light casualties. The regiment spent the next few weeks in billets at Hazebrouck, well to the rear, as a winter of frost, snow and intense cold tightened its grip. To brighten a dull routine the officers arranged for hounds – two each from the Quorn and Cottesmore hunts and one from the Fernie – to be brought over from Leicestershire to hunt hares and a drag. But such distractions could not disguise the fact that proud cavalrymen such as George Ball had landed in a foot-sloggers' war.

At the beginning of February 1915 the cavalry took over a sector from the French in the Ypres salient, which meant the regiment had to provide dismounted troops for duty in the trenches while leaving others behind to take charge of the horses. The Leicestershire Yeomanry would soon face its toughest test to date. The second battle for Ypres got under way on 22 April with the Germans using poisonous chlorine gas for the first time. At midnight on 12 May the regiment sent dismounted troops – fourteen officers and 247 men drawn from all three squadrons – into the line near Frezenberg, east of Ypres. The trenches were in bad condition, offering scant cover from shell fire, and the men started digging. As it grew light just before 4am the enemy opened up with a terrific bombardment of shrapnel and high-explosive shells. The shelling continued intermittently most of the day, with men blown up or buried as whole sections of trench were obliterated. B and C Squadrons, in what was left of the front line, came under attack from German troops who swept into the trenches on their flank. Without trench bombs or grenades to answer the enemy and with mud jamming their rifle bolts, the valiant Leicestershire men fell back from traverse to traverse until the survivors eventually reached the positions of the 3rd Dragoon Guards. Meanwhile A Squadron, in the support trenches, had begun to retire until Lieutenant

George Ball (standing far left) with Leicestershire Yeomanry comrades before being sent overseas in 1914. Below: George, now an officer, with family and friends, probably shortly after the war. Sister Evelyn has her arm round him. Sister Jessie is standing behind her. Elsie Ball is third from right in middle row

Colonel Evans-Freke emerged from his dugout and shouted, 'Hold hard', bringing them to a halt.

By holding out, A Squadron blocked the one gap open to the Germans to advance on Ypres. When fresh troops came up from the rear the squadron's forty survivors joined the attack, cheering wildly as they drove the enemy back in a bayonet charge. By the evening of 13 May the regiment had lost seven officers killed, including Evans-Freke, and eighty-seven other ranks killed or missing. It is not certain whether George Ball was with B Squadron in the front line or with the horses to the rear. But on 14 May he was promoted corporal.

The regiment was sent back to billets to rest, refit and train new drafts from England. George was struck by influenza in August 1915 but rapidly recovered. In the following months the regiment alternated between infantry work, repairing defences and training on horseback ready for cavalry operations should the hoped-for breakthrough come. Ball had recently been promoted sergeant when, in June 1916, the Leicestershire Yeomanry made a series of night rides to join other cavalry units at Corbie-sur-Somme in the lead-up to the great Somme offensive. The massively costly opening attack of 1 July failed to provide a gap for the cavalry to exploit. There were no glorious charges, only battlefield detritus to be cleared and more trenches to be repaired.

The regiment then moved to billets well in the rear and cheered themselves by staging a point-to-point meeting. In April 1917 there was a move to Arras, again in the hope of a crucial breakthrough. The Yeomanry had a close call when it rode through Monchy le Preux, a village supposedly cleared of the enemy but, in fact, containing German machine-gunners. The regiment got through with few casualties but the streets were choked with dead horses.

Ball had been singled out as officer material and, now allocated the regimental number 255089, he applied on 6 September 1917 for a temporary commission. He gave his preference as the cavalry or Royal Artillery and cited John Entwisle as a reference. Ball left France on 3 October and was posted to the 3rd Reserve Cavalry Regiment at Aldershot pending his transfer to No 1 Cavalry Cadet School. He made the move to that establishment, at Netheravon, on 28 February 1918. While on leave at some stage George had met Elsie Shufflebottom, daughter of a glass and china dealer from Manchester. She was visiting Leicestershire with her father, who was negotiating to buy a farm on the Lutterworth side of North Kilworth for his son, invalided out of the war. George, aged twenty-two, and twenty-seven-year-old Elsie were married by Mr Cox in North Kilworth on Tuesday 14 May 1918. The bridegroom, immaculate in uniform, had paid ten shillings (50p) for a special licence. The church was full but the celebrations were overshadowed, for close family at least, by concern over the welfare of George's brother Victor, taken prisoner in France.

Back at cadet school, Ball did well and a report on his performance concluded, 'Good command, should do well as an officer'. He scored good marks for his horsemanship, handling of sword and revolver while mounted and map-reading. His foot drill and grasp of military law were rated 'very fair'. He was granted a temporary commission as a second lieutenant on 29 August and joined the 4th Reserve Regiment of Dragoons at Aldershot on 18 September. The war, however, was nearly over and the army would soon be in less need of cavalry officers. Ball, every inch the cavalryman with neat moustache and highly polished boots as he attended the ex-servicemen's fete in 1919, was released from military duties that year.

He returned to help in his father's business. But there were difficult times ahead; the Depression hit sales and cheap steel trailer wheels with pneumatic tyres decreased demand for the wheelwright's craft. Men eventually had to be laid off. Away from work worries, George was a keen pigeon-fancier and won cups galore. For years he chaired the ex-servicemen's supper at the White Lion. Like many of his old comrades, he served in the Home Guard during the Second World War and as late as the 1960s he still read a lesson at the remembrance service each November. He stood down from the parish council in 1955 after twenty-four years.

George and Elsie, who had two daughters, marked their golden wedding quietly at home in North Kilworth in 1968. In later years George had worked for Johnson Brothers, contractors. Elsie died in 1970 and George went to live with his daughters in Poynton, Cheshire. Daughter Joan recalled, 'He never spoke of the war to us and he never rode again after he came home although he had the opportunity.' George adjusted to life away from Kilworth and enjoyed working in the garden, continuing to do so until a few months before his death aged ninety-two on 24 May 1988. The Poynton branch of the Royal British Legion, of which he was a member, ensured the Union Flag was draped on his coffin. It was a deserved tribute for one of the last survivors of those named on the North Kilworth memorial.

J. T. BENNETT

JAMES Thomas Bennett was the son of Cave Bennett, a North Kilworth farm labourer, and his wife Eliza. He was born on 6 June 1880 and baptised later that year by Rector Belgrave. James had an elder brother and sister and the family, who lived in Back Street, were related to the Morley family, who were to send two sons to the Great War. James started at North Kilworth school in June 1885 and later worked as a groom and gardener. As a youth he was a member of the village's air rifle team.

Little has emerged about his war service but by the end of 1917 he was an army corporal stationed at Thornhill Camp, Aldershot. He wrote to Kilworth just before Christmas to thank villagers for the gift parcel that he, like others, had been sent. James found the pork pie and cake a particular treat. He wrote, 'They have moved some of our lads over to France...I don't think it looks like the war being over for a long time. They keep sending a lot of troops from here and others keep coming in.' It is not known if James was sent overseas.

After the war he went back to being a gardener, an occupation he kept until retirement. In later years he moved to South Kilworth with his wife Alice. He died at the age of seventy-six on 3 March 1957 and was buried at North Kilworth.

J. BIRT

THE Burts were a family of Romany origin and lived in an ornate caravan in a field just east of the White Lion. The name was often written as Birt and appears on the war memorial spelt that way but Burt became the more usual form. Joseph Burt enlisted in the army on 10 December 1915 and initially served in the Leicestershire Regiment. However he was transferred to The King's Own (Royal Lancaster Regiment) as Private 27931. Joe was wounded, with shrapnel in his shoulder, and also lost some toes. His injuries were sufficiently serious for him to be honourably discharged on 14 September 1918.

After the war he worked in haulage and as a general dealer. Joe's wife, formerly Alice Smith, is thought to have hailed from the Towcester area. The couple had two sons and five daughters, at least some of whom married

Joe Burt, who was wounded, with his wife Alice and Joe junior

locally. Joe Burt was only forty-six when he died on 8 March 1924 after bronchitis led to complications. He is buried in North Kilworth churchyard. His son Bill was wounded serving in the RAF during the Second World War. He was a rear gunner on Halifax bombers before transferring to transport aircraft.

W. T. BURBIDGE

WOUNDED twice in four years of army service, Will Burbidge faced the task of readjusting to civilian life with the same determination that had helped him through painful and wearying weeks in hospital. Through it all he was supported by the devoted sweetheart who became his wife. From adversity came happiness.

William Thomas Burbidge, born on 19 January 1895, was given the christian names of his father when he was baptised at North Kilworth on 5 May that year. He was the first child of William senior, a blacksmith at Ball's who hailed from Foleshill in Warwickshire, and his wife Catherine Elizabeth, usually called Lizzie, originally from Welford. The couple had another son, Mansell, who became head gardener at Kilworth House. Born in 1902,

Mansell was too young to serve in the Great War. There was also a daughter Amy who, as Mrs Mattock, kept a small shop in Kilworth. A baby boy Arthur, born between Will and Mansell, did not survive.

Little William – Will to his family but often called Willie – started at Kilworth school on 14 April 1899. In 1907 he was guard to George Stock's king at the May Day celebrations. At the annual pupils' treat that year he took first prize for attendance and conduct in Class I of the Sunday school. His diligence in scripture studies also impressed Miss Ada Belgrave, a daughter of Kilworth's late Rector, as she presented him with a Bible in 1908.

Will went to work as a carpenter and joiner at the Rugby building firm of Frederick George Rainbow, signing his apprenticeship papers on 9 January 1911. He was paid a penny three farthings (less than 1p) an hour. Will went to live in Barby, south of Rugby, and started courting Eleanor Edith Harris, always known as Edie. She was born in Hackney, East London, but she and a younger sister had returned to Barby with their parents when their father, a London policeman and fireman, became ill. When she was old enough Edie went back to London where she worked as a cashier for the Home & Colonial stores.

The Great War had been underway for just over four months when Will, a little under 5ft 6in tall, went to Northampton to volunteer on 17 December 1914. His apprenticeship had until 1916 to run but his country's needs took prior claim over those of his employer. Will became a private in the Northamptonshire Regiment. By the time the war ended he had been transferred to The Queen's (Royal West Surrey Regiment), the Labour Corps, back to the Northamptonshire Regiment and finally to the Royal Engineers, with a change of regimental number each time. It was not unusual for a soldier to be switched between units because of casualties or organisational needs but Private Burbidge's moves seem exceptional and may have been brought on in part by his absences through wounds.

He had been in the army only a matter of weeks when he was first wounded in February or March 1915 somewhere in France. The details are sketchy but his family believes he was shot then pulled to safety by an officer. The local press reported he had been wounded in the arm and leg. Will was brought back to Bishop's Knoll (2nd Southern General) Hospital at Stoke Bishop, Bristol. From there he sent a postcard to his 'Darling Edie', then living in Dalston, East London, reassuring her he was 'getting on nicely' and promising to reply to her letter as soon as he had writing paper and stamps.

Will and Edie Burbidge on their wedding day in August 1918

Will Burbidge (rear, second from right) in a Bristol hospital

It is not known when Will was returned to active service but he was next wounded late in 1917, probably from shrapnel. (His discharge certificate listed wound scars on his left hip, shoulder and chest.) A padre at the casualty clearing station wrote to Will's mother to tell her his condition was improving and he was expected to be fit enough to be moved to the base in two or three days. Luckily this time he was sent to a hospital much nearer home, in Leicester. He had to spend Christmas there but was cheered by the arrival of a gift parcel from the Kilworth parishioners. On 21 December he sent a thank-you letter saying, 'They are busy decorating our ward up today and I think we shall have a very good Christmas.' He predicted his recovery would be 'a slow job' and again it is not known when he returned to service. He was in uniform when, aged twenty-three, he married twenty-one-year-old Edie at the parish church in Hillmorton, near Rugby, on 5 August 1918.

At the end of the war Will was Pioneer 207129 in a waterways and railways unit of the Royal Engineers. At about the time of the Armistice he was apparently on leave and able to take Edie to North Kilworth where Rector Cox and his sister Alice met the new Mrs Burbidge for the first time. 'They all seem to think the world of you,' Will's proud mother wrote to her soldier son afterwards. Will was finally released from the army as being no longer physically fit for war service, although the war had been over three months by the time of his official discharge on 21 February 1919. He was granted a disability pension but lost it when he got back to work. He and Edie had two sons and a daughter.

Like so many veterans, Will Burbidge spoke very little of his army experiences and never complained about the misfortunes that the war had brought him. He died at his Hillmorton home on 6 November 1966 and is remembered in the family as a man of strong principles coupled with an easygoing and tolerant manner, 'a lovely man, a real gentleman with great kindness and courtesy'.

G. BUSWELL

HE was among the last and youngest to leave North Kilworth for the army but George Frederick Buswell 'did his bit' as willingly as any of the men who went before. It was not easy for him or his parents as his elder brother Joe had died in the war. Joe is honoured on the war memorial at Welford.

George was born at South Kilworth on 19 January 1900. His father Joseph worked as a farm labourer and shepherd. Joseph and his wife Emma had previously lived in Welford and did so again soon after George's birth. George was to earn his place on the memorial at North Kilworth because, for at least some of his childhood, he lived with the family of his mother's brother George Stapleton in that village. One of the Stapleton children, Alf, is also named on the memorial. George Buswell went to South Kilworth school but in 1907 he and his younger brother Frederick moved to North Kilworth school, though for how long is unknown.

George, whose particular pals included David Dorman, another future soldier, was working as a wagoner on a farm when he attested at Leicester on 14 February 1918, giving his address as North Kilworth. He had celebrated his eighteenth birthday only twenty-five days previously. His brother Joe, who served in the Royal Fusiliers, had died of wounds in France on 20 February 1917. George was enlisted in the 53rd (Young Soldier) Battalion of the Leicestershire Regiment and sent to Rugeley Camp in Staffordshire. Three months later he was posted to the regiment's 51st (Graduated)

Young George Buswell in 1918

George with wife-to-be Doris

Battalion in Nottinghamshire. The Leicesters were one of several regiments that, regardless of their own numbering system, had battalions designated 53rd for eighteen-year-old recruits and 51st and 52nd for soldiers who had completed basic training.

The war had been over for nearly four months when Buswell crossed the Channel to Dunkirk on 8 March 1919 on his way to become a member of the forces occupying conquered German territory as the British Army of the Rhine, a term brought into use again after the Second World War. That July his transfer to the No 2 Company Midland Division Training, Royal Army Service Corps, as a driver on horse transport was confirmed. The ASC, unkindly dubbed Ally Sloper's Cavalry after a comic strip character of the period, had been awarded its Royal prefix in recognition of the prodigious feats of logistics it performed during the war. Buswell was sent home on 3 September and finally granted his discharge on 18 December as Driver 452396 of 537 Company RASC.

After the war George lived at South Kilworth and was a handyman at Kilworth House. He later worked for J. Parnell and Sons, builders in Rugby, and cycled there daily, stopping off to feed his hens. He was with the firm for thirty-one years. George met his wife Doris at a cricket match in Dunton Bassett, her home village, and they married in 1924 at Lutterworth where they made their home. The couple, who had no children, celebrated their golden wedding anniversary in 1974 when both were aged seventy-four.

A hard worker who did not retire until 1968, George spent much of his leisure time gardening and won a hundred cups at local horticultural shows over the years. He died on 26 February 1981, aged eighty-one. His funeral on 5 March was held at North Kilworth, the village from where he went to serve his country sixty-three years before.

C. CARTER

WILLIAM and Eliza Carter had three sons in uniform during the Great War – Charles, Edward and Leonard. Charles was born at North Kilworth on 12 October 1887. At the time his father worked as a labourer but was later employed operating an engine in a sawmill. Charles was baptised at St Andrew's in May 1888. He started at Kilworth school on 19 October 1891. In an attempt to prevent a measles outbreak, Charles was kept from lessons on doctor's orders for a few days when he was ten after his younger brother Len was struck by the illness.

Charlie worked as a labourer in a timber yard but became a painter at Ball's and was a member of the village's minstrel troupe alongside his boss George Ball. He was aged twenty-six when a recruiting sergeant signed him up at Welford on 7 September 1914, barely a month after the outbreak of war. Charlie expected to go into the Northamptonshire Regiment but for some reason he was posted to the East Surrey Regiment. After training he crossed the Channel on 6 March 1915 to join the 2nd Battalion. Recalled from India at the end of 1914, the battalion had been sent to France as part of 85th Brigade 28th Division in January 1915. It was not long before Charlie was in the thick of it.

As the Second Battle of Ypres got under way the battalion took heavy casualties in attempts to drive the Germans out of trenches near Zonnebeke on 26 April. The toll of deaths and injuries continued to rise steadily into the following month. On 2 May Carter's battalion saw a greenish yellow veil hanging over the trenches a little along the line near St Julien. It was the Germans' vile new weapon, chlorine gas. The battalion moved back to billets a mile east of Poperinghe after a few days and there they were inspected by the divisional and corps commanders before taking up new positions in the line. On 8 May the battalion received orders to move astride the Ypres-Zonnebeke road and retake trenches at Frezenberg. The troops passed through a gap in the entanglement in front of the line and advanced at 4pm. Many men fell as German machine-gunners raked them with fire from a farm on the battalion's left front. Heavy shelling added to the nightmare. One company south of the road advanced to reinforce the East Yorkshires in a trench east of Verlorenhoek but could advance no further. The battalion held the line throughout the next day despite enduring a heavy bombardment in the afternoon. It was about that time that Carter was shot in the arm. As he was taken back for treatment the East Surreys were moved and the Cavalry Brigade prepared to take over the position. The brigade included the Leicestershire Yeomanry. Carter did not know it but he might have come within a mile or so of George Ball and Ted Cheney from North Kilworth, soldiers in the Yeomanry.

Private 3104 Carter was on his way home on 13 May as the Yeomanry faced a ferocious German onslaught (*see G. Ball, this chapter*). He was sent to a hospital in Manchester to recover and was then transferred to the East Surrey Regiment's 3rd (Reserve) Battalion based at Dover. In the October he was moved to the 4th (Extra Reserve) Battalion in Saltash, Cornwall. The army needed every man and on 10 December 1915 he was sent back to France to join the 7th (Service) Battalion. Carter was shot again on 10 April 1917, though the details and extent of the wound are unclear. Certainly the injury was serious enough for him to be returned to Britain for a long stay at the Abram Peel War Hospital in Bradford. He was eventually sent home from hospital in the November and was discharged from the army on 1 December as no longer fit for war service. Charlie received his Silver War Badge and certificate before Christmas. The individually numbered badge proved that the man wearing it on the lapel of his civilian jacket had played his part in the war.

Charlie was allowed a pension of 27s 6d (£1.37p) for four weeks after which it dropped to 19s 3d (96p) for thirteen weeks, then 11s (55p) subject to review. In any case he got his job back at Ball's and continued to work for the firm for many years. On 9 December 1918 he married Sarah Jane

Dorman, always known as Addy from her third christian name Adelaide. She was the sister of John Dorman, who had died in France *(see J. Dorman, The Fallen)*. The couple lived in Tudor Cottages, previously known as Billet Cottages, North Kilworth. Charlie served in the Home Guard during the Second World War. He died, aged seventy-three, on 12 February 1961.

E. W. CARTER

EDWARD William Carter was the eldest son of William and Eliza Carter. He was born at North Kilworth on 10 April 1878 and between him and Charles, subject of the previous entry, there were two other brothers Henry and Alfred. Edward, baptised on 11 August 1878, started at Kilworth school when he was five. When he left he worked as an errand boy but by 1911 he was a waiter at the East India United Service Club in St James's, London. Edward was one of many servants employed to cater for the members, who were East India Company staff on leave or army and navy officers who had served in India. Details of Edward's later employment and war service have not come to light.

L. J. CARTER

YOUNGEST of the Carter brothers, Leonard John was born in 1891 and was baptised at North Kilworth on 20 March 1892. He followed his brothers in attending Kilworth school. In April 1904 the pupils staged an entertainment of songs, recitations and a sketch entitled *Matrimonee* in which Len played one of the 'grumbling husbands'. He was a keen sportsman, playing for the village's football and cricket teams. An early hint of his enthusiasm came when he managed second place in an eighty-yards race for under-eights at the children's treat and sports at Kilworth House in June 1899.

Len was a farm labourer before the Great War. He is said to have served in the Leicestershire Regiment, though it is possible he was transferred to the Army Service Corps and later the Royal Engineers. Len, who never married, later became a council roadman, a job he kept until retirement. He lived with his brother Charlie and his wife at Tudor Cottages, where he died on 8 June 1965 at the age of seventy-four.

A. W. CHENEY

THREE Cheney brothers went to the Great War. All eventually returned home but not before the youngest, Will, had been seriously wounded and spent sixteen months as a prisoner of the Germans. He, Ted and Allen were the sons of Thomas and Emma Cheney. Thomas, who sported a red beard, was a policeman who had served elsewhere in Leicestershire before arriving in North Kilworth. After leaving the force he became an insurance agent and later worked on a farm. An elder son, John, worked as a boy at Wykes's bakery and later became a policeman in Birmingham. There were ten Cheney children in all, although four died young.

Will was born at Kilworth on 4 November 1896 and was christened Alfred William at St Andrew's on 27 December. He rarely used his first name and even at school he was logged as William. He started in the infants class at Kilworth on 9 March 1900, the same day as Victor Ball *(see V. E. Ball, The Fallen)*. He left in July 1909 along with two other future soldiers, George Stock and William Pebody. Will worked for a while as a pot boy at the Red Lion, Sibbertoft, over the border in Northamptonshire, but by 1915 he was a gardener for the Entwisles at Kilworth House, earning £1 3s 4d (£1.17) a fortnight.

It is not certain when he joined up but in 1916, the year after his father died, Will was Private 45542 in the 14th (Service) Battalion of the Durham Light Infantry. The proud DLI was to finish the Great War with six Victoria Crosses to its credit at the cost of more than 12,500 casualties. Will was still only nineteen when he was sent to France on 25 July 1916. By March 1917 his battalion, a component of the 6th Division, was at the front near Loos, scene of the 1915 battle amid the coalfields of northern France. It was a perilous spot with raids, counter-raids and lots of artillery and trench mortar activity. On 13 April – shortly after the Canadians took Vimy Ridge, further south – the Germans started to pull back from their lines opposite part of the 6th Division's front. The British guns pounded the enemy trenches and the infantry grabbed as much ground as possible without committing itself to a serious battle. This continued for four days until the Germans evidently decided they had retreated farther than they meant to and became worried about holding the redoubt known as Hill 70, east of Loos. They stiffened their opposition and several British infantry units became involved in intense fighting.

Will Cheney as a young soldier in the Durham Light Infantry

On 20 April the 14th DLI went into the line, occupying a position known as Netley Trench, north of Lens. Next day the battalion attacked, supported by rifle grenade and Lewis gun fire. The Durhams seized German trenches and took thirty-five prisoners and two machine-guns. An officer and eighteen men crawled out through some ruined houses to knock out a strong point where previous attacks had failed. Few casualties were suffered during the attack but the battalion was heavily hit by shelling before and after the fight.

At 8am on 22 April two companies of the Durhams advanced to take a trench called Nash Alley and a redoubt known as the Dynamite Magazine. It was part of a bigger attack with troops on either flank joining in. A shrapnel barrage from British gunners meant the Durhams were on the Germans before they could get their machine-guns into action and the objectives were taken. A counter-attack was beaten off and the battalion started to consolidate the captured positions. Unfortunately the British artillery had flattened most of the trenches and the Dynamite Magazine consisted of one dug-out and a heap of earth. It left little cover from German snipers and machine-gunners firing from houses in Cité St Laurent, near Lens. Two counter-attacks were repulsed. The Durhams, though weak in numbers, kept up the struggle even after a heavy German barrage and further attack. But finally they had to give ground and fell back slowly, still fighting hard.

Only three badly wounded men were left in the hands of the enemy. One of them was Will Cheney. As his comrades were relieved and sent back behind the lines his fate lay in the hands of German doctors. His captors took him to the village of Annoeullin, near Lille, where he was treated for a broken right arm and wounds to his head, legs, shoulder and hand. After a few weeks he was moved to Lille and then on to Tournai, Belgium, where many other British prisoners were being held. He was there for about ten days before he joined about 250 PoWs on the two-day journey into Germany. Will arrived at Dulmen camp hospital in western Germany on 2 June. He remained in hospital until 2 February 1918 when he was fit enough to move into the camp itself.

The following month Will's mother received reassuring news about his progress in captivity. Another soldier, Arthur Cross, who had befriended Will in Dulmen, contacted Mrs Cheney from his Bristol home after he had been repatriated under exchange arrangements. Cross wrote, 'Up to the time I left

Will Cheney (seated centre) with other prisoners of war

the camp he was quite well. He was one of the happiest lads in the camp, always laughing and making the best of captivity. You will be glad to know he had been receiving his food parcels regularly and I may say one can live quite comfortably on them, not wanting any more German food.'

By the time the letter arrived Will had been transferred to Friedrichsfeld camp. On 10 May he was sent to Wessel where a doctor examined him with a view to him being sent back to Britain. But it was 8 August before he finally left Friedrichsfeld. At Aachen he was again examined and passed for transit to England via neutral Holland. He was put on a ship at Rotterdam and after two days at sea was home on 18 August. Will took back with him a piece of black bread given to him by a friendly Russian PoW. Ninety years later that memento of his captivity was still preserved by the Cheney family. Will still needed treatment for his wounds and spent some time at King George's Hospital in Stamford Street, London. After the war he lived with his mother at Billet Cottages. He was thirty-one when he married Violet Tanser at South Kilworth church on 9 April 1928. Violet was the widow of John Tanser, a wartime Army Service Corps driver, who had died in 1923. Will, who worked at Kilworth House for nearly fifty years, was a great lover of nature and the local countryside. He and Violet had no children. Will had been widowed for six years when he died at his North Kilworth home on 26 August 1974, aged seventy-seven. Among the mourners at his funeral was his pal, fellow gardening enthusiast and former Great War soldier George Buswell.

A. F. CHENEY

MENTION of the Great War conjures up images of mud and barbed wire on the Western Front and, of course, many of North Kilworth's soldiers did serve in France and Belgium. Allen Cheney, however, was a member of the army that fought in the arduous and dangerous, although largely forgotten, Salonica campaign.

Allen Frederick Cheney was born in North Kilworth on 27 September 1894 and baptised at St Andrew's on 2 December. He was the younger brother of Ted and elder brother of Will *(see previous entry)*. Allen started at the village school on 24 June 1898. As an eleven-year-old in December 1905 he earned a severe telling-off along with Leonard Wearing when, having being allowed out with the rest of the school to see the hounds, the pair failed to return to lessons on time. He left school in 1907 and was an errand boy for a while. He later moved to Rugby where he trained as a butcher. Most likely he would have continued in the trade uninterrupted had it not been for the Great War. However, just shy of his twentieth birthday, Allen enlisted at Rugby on 15 September 1914. He became Private 13576 in the newly formed 12th (Service) Battalion of the Hampshire Regiment. The battalion was a component of K3, part of Kitchener's volunteer New Army.

Allen Cheney served in the Hampshire Regiment in Salonica

Cheney arrived in France with his battalion on 21 September 1915 but the Hampshires were not destined for the front. On 15 November they embarked on the SS Canada at Marseilles, arriving at Salonica ten days later. What were British troops doing sailing up the Aegean to land at this port (now Thessaloniki) in neutral Greece? To the north an Austro-German force had invaded Serbia, overwhelming all opposition. British and French forces were sent to Serbia's defence. To complicate matters, the Austrians also invaded Serbia's ally and neighbour Montenegro. Bulgaria, eager to annex the southern Serb region of Macedonia, also attacked the Serbs.

Salonica was essential as a base for the French and British expedition and from there they pushed forward until an Allied line was established from the Adriatic in the west, via Monastir, across to Lake Doiran then down to the east of Stavros on the Aegean. This line, with minor variations, was to remain for the whole of 1916 and 1917. The Bulgarians hid away in an inaccessible area of mountain passes, steep gorges and few roads. British troops attempting to confront them were hampered by supply problems. Over the last fourteen miles from the Salonica base to one point in the British line everything had to be carried by mules. But by far the worst hindrance was malaria. It was said that ten times as many British soldiers entered hospital with malaria as with wounds and it is thought that Allen Cheney was among them. Mosquito nets were in limited supply and the only (temporary) remedy was a dose of quinine. An outbreak of sandy fever in July 1917 and the Spanish flu of 1918 added to the miseries. Of a total of 9,717 British deaths in Salonica, 55 per cent were from disease and accidents.

However, in September 1918 the Allies struck hard, with Cheney's battalion taking part in its own last operation. It beat the Bulgarians at White Scar Hill, just west of Lake Doiran, and followed them as they retreated into Serbia. Bulgaria pulled out of the war and the Hampshires, severely reduced in strength, took up occupation duties. It is uncertain when Cheney returned home but by May 1919 he had left the army. Four months later his old battalion had ceased to exist.

Allen married Annie Shone in 1921 and the couple had one son and two daughters. Allen continued as a butcher in New Bilton, Rugby, and was still working at the age of seventy. He died on 26 June 1966. Allen Cheney's 1914-15 Star, British War Medal and Victory Medal remain in his family, neatly framed with the metal shoulder titles of the Hampshire Regiment.

E. B. CHENEY

T HE Army Service Corps was pleased to have a volunteer like Bert Cheney. With his five-year apprenticeship as a wheelwright completed at Ball's, he was the sort of man needed to keep the Corps's largely horse-drawn supply wagons rolling. Many a young chap joining the recruiting rush in August 1914 pictured himself wielding a rifle in the local infantry regiment. But a soldier without bullets for his weapon and without food in his belly was no soldier at all – which is where the ASC came in. At its wartime peak the Corps had more than 10,500 officers and 315,000 men plus tens of thousands of Indian, Egyptian, Chinese and other non-British labourers toiling to deliver the masses of equipment and supplies essential to an army in the field.

Bert was born at North Kilworth in June 1890, the son of Edwin Cheney, a blacksmith's striker at Ball's, and his wife Eliza, of Station Road. Christened Edwin Bertie on July 20, Bert was unrelated to the three Cheney brothers whose names appear with his on the village memorial. As a youth he played in the pre-war village football team, which included several other future soldiers, and attended social events at the Belgrave Memorial Hall. Bert was twenty-four when, exactly a week into the war, he joined the army on 11 August 1914. He signed up at the Service Corps's No 2 Depot at Woolwich, south-east London, where he had no difficulty passing the trade proficiency test in the workshops a few days later. It is not known if Cheney already had London connections which prompted him to volunteer there but his future wife was from a suburb of the capital.

Bert was sent to France on 5 November 1914 as Wheeler/Driver TS/786 in No 4 Company of the ASC's 8th Divisional Train. Wheeler was the army term for a wheelwright. The 8th Division remained on the Western Front throughout the war: at Neuve Chapelle and Aubers in 1915, on the Somme in 1916, during the German retreat to the Hindenburg Line and at Third Ypres in 1917 and on the Somme and at the Battles of the Aisne and Arras in 1918. Cheney's records make no mention of him transferring to any other unit so it is reasonable to assume he was involved in the support efforts for at least some of these battles. He was promoted wheeler corporal in December 1915.

Cheney was granted two weeks' leave in June 1917 but by the end of the year he was understandably suffering a touch of war weariness. When he wrote to Kilworth's parishioners in December to thank them for the gift parcel he had received he said, 'It is very nice to think that you are not quite forgotten by old friends after being so long away from them, but I hope the time will not be long before I shall see you all again and this terrible war finished.' It would be more than a year before Bert could leave the army for ever but he was allowed home for two weeks in January 1918. On the 17th he married gardener's daughter Alice Edworthy at her local church in Surbiton, Surrey. Then it was back to France. Bert survived the war physically unscathed, apart from accidentally cutting his right hand in September 1918. He was sent back to Britain from Ghislenghien in Belgium in March 1919 and was finally discharged on 24 April. At the time his home address was given as Tolworth, Surbiton. Details of Cheney's life after the war have not emerged. His parents continued to live in North Kilworth.

E. W. CHENEY

THE first of the three Cheney brothers to go to war, and the oldest, was Ted. Having become a part-time cavalryman in the Leicestershire Yeomanry in 1913, he was mobilised as soon as hostilities broke out in August 1914 and served throughout the conflict.

Edward Wilford Cheney was born at North Kilworth on 14 June 1892, the son of Thomas and Emma Cheney *(see A. W. Cheney, this chapter)*. When he was baptised at St Andrew's on 14 August Edward was given his mother's maiden name as his second name. In April 1899 the *Rugby Advertiser* reported how a little son of Thomas Cheney was running behind a milk cart and holding on to it as it headed to the station at Kilworth when he suddenly let go. He tumbled into the path of another milk cart following rapidly behind. The boy was knocked down and a wheel went partly over him but luckily no bones were broken. 'A marvellous escape', the newspaper said. 'It should act as a warning to youngsters.' A local resident carried the shaken lad a quarter of a mile home. The unnamed Cheney boy was said to be seven years old and as Edward was only two months short of his seventh birthday at the time it seems likely he was the little daredevil.

Edward attended the village school where he was perhaps not the keenest scholar. As a nine-year-old he was sent home for persisting in returning late after the lunch break. Whatever his attitude to lessons, Edward

Ted Cheney, a sergeant farrier, with his bride Alice in 1918

Ted Cheney (rear, second from right) in the Leics Yeomanry

was to prove a valuable worker for Ball's as a smith and farrier at the forge next to Billet Cottages, down the slope from the firm's main premises. His duties sometimes took him to farms to shoe horses or repair plough shares and other equipment.

Cheney joined the Leicestershire Yeomanry, part of the cavalry arm of the Territorial Force, as did his workmates George Ball junior and Walter Morley. Ted's regimental number 1947 was only three later than that of George's. Private Cheney arrived in France with his comrades on 2 November 1914 and soon came under fire, making him eligible for a clasp to his 1914 Star campaign medal. The Princess Mary's gift tin that he received that Christmas is pictured on the back cover of this book. Ted served as a farrier in the Yeomanry and in later years recalled coming across a horse lost or abandoned by the enemy. He trimmed its hooves and shoed it and the animal was soon in use with the British Army. Ted reckoned the horse later recognised him and neighed when he came near. At some stage of the war Cheney was billeted on a farm where he was treated to stew and thick chunks of bread by the farmer's wife.

Ted Cheney (third from left) watching other farriers at work

Ted Cheney's story from 1914 to early 1917 is essentially the same as that of George Ball, namely an often gruelling and dangerous time as the Yeomanry served in mounted and dismounted roles outside Ypres, on the Somme and in the Arras sector *(see G. Ball, this chapter)*. However, when Ball left the Yeomanry for officer training in 1917, Cheney continued with the regiment and was later promoted farrier sergeant.

The regiment had lost many horses at Arras in 1917 and was pulled well back way out of harm's way to a spot called Dominois, fifteen miles north of Abbeville, to await the arrival of replacement mounts. While at Dominois the officers were invited to join the local boar hunt and had a good gallop through the Forêt de Crécy. In June the Yeomanry were on the move again, to Tincourt, east of Péronne, in an area left devastated by the Germans when they retired over the previous winter. The cavalrymen were soon hard at work in an infantry role, improving trenches and wire in a section of line at Epehy near the Canal de St Quentin. Spirits remained high although the regiment suffered casualties when the Germans mounted a determined raid on its position. August brought another move, this time to billets at Guarbecque, north-east of Béthune. While there the regiment took part in a divisional horse show and No 4 troop of Cheney's B Squadron took the prize for the best troop of men and horses.

Later in the year the regiment joined a cavalry concentration on the Cambrai front. But hopes of a wholesale breakthrough with cavalry galloping through the gap in the enemy front came to nothing. In November the regiment was moved yet again to occupy trenches near St Quentin on the extreme right of the British Fifth Army front. In January 1918 the Leicestershire Yeomanry's days as a cohesive cavalry unit were coming to an end with the men again employed digging support and reserve trenches. The army was suffering acute manpower shortages and in March orders came through for the Leicestershire Yeomanry to hand over it horses ready for conversion to a dismounted machine-gun battalion. However, when several regular cavalry units were mauled at the start of the German spring offensive it was reckoned to be more sensible to use the Yeomanry to fill the gaps thus left. On 4 April the regiment was split up with Cheney and his B Squadron comrades being assimilated into the 16th Lancers. Within days the 3rd Cavalry Brigade, of which Cheney's new unit was a part, was rushed north to take up reserve positions after a German attack on the River Lys. In July the brigade moved back to Etaples for training.

By then, however, Cheney had been granted home leave. Smart in uniform, he married twenty-four-year-old Ivy Alice Macnamara at St Andrew's, North Kilworth, on Wednesday 19 June 1918. The bride, born in central London and always known as Alice, was one of Mrs Kenna's domestic servants at the Hall. She would have caught Ted's eye before the war as she cleaned the steps while he walked past on his way from Ball's main premises to the forge or to his mother's nearby cottage. Alice had previously worked for a naval officer's family in Hampshire.

Back in France the 3rd Cavalry Brigade took part in the Battle of Amiens, attacks on the Hindenburg Line and the general advance towards Mons. In the closing stages of the war the fighting at last broke free of the trenches and the former Yeomanry men were finally able to act as cavalry on the battlefield. It is not certain when Cheney returned to the Lancers after his leave and how much of this action he saw. But at Christmas 1918 he sent home a card produced by the 2nd Cavalry Division, of which the Lancers were part. It featured a drawing of a hapless German soldier being sent headlong by a kick from the rear hooves of a cavalry mount. The caption read 'The Hun's Retirement according to plan'.

After the war the newlyweds lived with Ted's mother for a while before moving to Church Street. When Ball's had to lay men off Ted found another job with E. Truelove and Sons, agricultural, electrical and general engineers of Railway Terrace, Rugby, where he worked for many years. He was a keen gardener in later years (his shallots took a prize at the horticultural show in 1927). Ted was on the committee of the village's ex-servicemen's club with his brother Will. He joined the Home Guard in the Second World War during which the Cheneys' daughter Kathleen served in the Women's Auxiliary Air Force and earned a Mention in Dispatches.

Ted attended the Leicestershire Yeomanry Association's dinner each year and was in Leicester for its golden jubilee reunion in 1970. By then he and Alice had celebrated their golden wedding. The couple moved to a bungalow in Elmcroft Road, North Kilworth, in later years. Aged eighty, Ted Cheney died there on 7 January 1973 a few weeks after Alice.

A. E. CLARKE

O NE of North Kilworth's first volunteers, Albert Clarke swapped a baker's apron for the uniform of an artilleryman. He obviously performed his military duties well as he was a sergeant by the time he was demobbed in 1919.

Albert Edward Clarke was born on 5 January 1893, one of seven children of James and Elizabeth Clarke. The family lived in Moulton, Northampton, at the time but later moved to Grosvenor Road, Rugby. Albert followed his father and elder brother William into the bakery trade and moved to North Kilworth some years before the Great War to work at the Co-op store in Cranmer Lane. Residents had contacted Rugby Co-operative Society about the possibility of establishing a branch in the village. Society representatives organised a tea and meeting in the summer of 1906 to explain the merits of the movement and a shop was duly opened.

Albert was twenty-one and unmarried when he went to Rugby on 8 September 1914 to enlist less than five weeks after war was declared. Whether boredom with the bakery or simple patriotism was his main motivation we do not know. Albert, a small chap at 5ft 4in and 9st 4lb, was accepted into the Royal Field Artillery and given the regimental number 11688. He was sent to France with A/79th Brigade. Details of his service have not come to light but he remained abroad for four years with periods of home leave. He was promoted sergeant on 7 November 1918, four days before the Armistice. He was able to show off his new stripes when he returned home on leave in May 1919 but before the end of the month his army service was over. Albert seems to have left North Kilworth before or around the time that Arthur Scobie took over as manager at the Co-op in about 1924.

B. J. CLARKE

BERT Clarke emigrated to Canada before the Great War and served in his adopted country's army. However, his name was included on North Kilworth's memorial along with his brother's because he was born and raised in the village and his parents still lived there.

Bertram John Clarke was the elder son of Thomas Measures Clarke and his wife Emily. The couple were prominent in village affairs. Thomas, a wheelwright and carpenter born in Lutterworth, was a church sidesman, school manager and overseer of the poor and served on the parish council and Belgrave Memorial Hall committee. With George Ball, he had been responsible for overseeing the contract for the building of the hall in 1902. Emily, a member of the Weston family of North Kilworth, was organist at St Andrew's for more than twenty years.

Bert was born on 18 December 1891 and baptised on 19 April the following year. Bertie, as he was known as an infant, attended Kilworth school and earned a mention in the *Rugby Advertiser* when, as a seven-year-old, he won the children's wild flowers section at the newly inaugurated flower and vegetable show in 1899. Bert worked for a while as a milling machinist for a firm of electrical engineers but he later trained as an accountant and in about 1911 he went to live in Canada. Come the Great War, Canada, like Australia and New Zealand, responded to the mother country's appeal for support. The victory at Vimy Ridge in April 1917 tells all that needs to be known about the courage and commitment of Canadian troops. In 1917 Canada agreed to Britain's request to introduce conscription.

Bert Clarke (rear) watching practice on a Canadian firing range

Bert Clarke in Canadian Army   **Bert at 60 in British Columbia**

Fair-haired Clarke was living in Lethbridge, Alberta, when he enlisted at Calgary, 110 miles to the north-west, on 3 May 1918. He became Gunner 3208802 in the 78th Depot Battery of the Canadian Expeditionary Force but transferred later that month to the 13th Battalion Canadian Garrison Regiment. By then army medics had discovered that Clarke had painful, congenital joint problems in his feet that ruled out marching. However, the army could still make use of an otherwise healthy young man and Clarke was even appointed acting sergeant on 23 July. He was transferred to the 1st Depot Battalion of the Alberta Regiment in the September. Clarke was never called on to serve abroad but he is said to have been involved in the grim duty of touring hospitals with a horse-drawn carriage to remove for burial those who had died in the flu pandemic.

After the war Clarke joined the British American Paint Co in Calgary and stayed with the firm for the whole of his working life. Initially he travelled throughout western Canada selling paint and brushes. On 19 August 1921 he was married to an English girl, Nellie, in Red Deer, north of Calgary. She had emigrated from Shotley, near Ipswich in Suffolk. The couple moved to Regina, Saskatchewan, where Clarke opened a warehouse and retail stores for his company and distributed paint products throughout the province. The couple's son and daughter were born in Regina. In about 1947 Clarke moved to head office in Victoria, British Columbia, and retired there in 1956. Bert Clarke died on 11 August 1982 at the age of 90.

W. T. CLARKE

WHEN North Kilworth honoured its soldiers with a fete in 1919 two men, proud in their crisp officers' uniforms, stood out from the crowd. One was George Ball, whose story has already been told. The other was Bill Clarke, commissioned as a second lieutenant in the artillery, but about to return to civilian status.

William Thomas Clarke was born on 30 September 1896, the younger son of Thomas and Emily Clarke *(see previous entry),* and was baptised at St Andrew's on 27 November that year. He attended Kilworth school, where he was known as Willie, and at the May Day celebrations in 1907 he was one of the guards to George Stock's king. In 1908 Willie left to go to the

Bill Clarke (right) with fiancée Marjorie Dimblebee at a wedding

Murray School in Rugby and the following year he was awarded top prize for his efforts at Sunday school in Kilworth. He was also a member of the church choir. Like his brother Bert, Bill was destined for a white collar career and was articled to Sam Robbins, the Rugby auctioneers.

He was nineteen when on 3 January 1916 he joined the Honourable Artillery Company, part of the Territorial Force. The HAC, formed in 1537, had a certain social prestige and the air of a club, so one might surmise that Clarke knew someone willing to pull strings to get him into such a unit. He attested at HAC headquarters at Armoury House, Finsbury, central London. As Driver 624526, he was posted to 2nd/A Battery (1st City of London Horse Artillery) HAC, formed in 1914 as a second line battery to 1st/A Battery. It became part of 126th Army Brigade Royal Field Artillery. Bill served in Britain until 21 June 1917 when he was sent to France where he drove horse-pulled gun carriages. At some stage he was made acting corporal. In October 1917, while still in France, Bill applied for a commission, giving as references the Rector and the head of the Murray School. In February 1918 he was recommended for admission as an officer cadet but continued serving in France until the end of July. He was then granted two weeks' home leave but had been back in France for only a fortnight when he was summoned to return to Britain to be attached as an officer cadet to 2nd Brigade Royal Field Artillery. On 11 October 1918 he was posted to No 1 RFA Officer Cadet School in St John's Wood, London. Clarke was appointed to his commission as a second lieutenant in the Royal Field Artillery on 9 April 1919. But, with the war over, he was never called upon to take up his duties and was discharged on 29 September that year.

Initially he returned to Kilworth and to his work as an auctioneer and on 30 January 1924 he married Marjorie Dimblebee, twenty-four-year-old daughter of Albert Dimblebee, a grocer from Husbands Bosworth. The church ceremony was in South Norwood, Surrey, where bride or groom had relatives. The couple's only child, a daughter, was born in 1925. Bill's professional expertise was in demand at a garden fete in the rectory orchard at Kilworth in July 1925 when he auctioned off left-over produce in aid of North Kilworth Nursing Association.

In about 1926 the family moved to Southend where, at the outbreak of the Second World War, Bill was working for Milner & Co, auctioneers and valuers. In the summer of 1940 his application for a commission in the Army Officers' Emergency Reserve was accepted. But he later declined an invitation to join an officer training unit in Yorkshire, citing business commitments. By 1941 he had moved to Rugby as a ministry official assessing claims for war damage to property. The work took him to Stafford and Leamington Spa and to Coventry, which had suffered severely in the bombing of November 1940. The offer of a commission was rescinded in September 1941.

After the war Bill returned to Southend until 1951 when he moved to Esher in Surrey. He worked for renowned estate agents Knight, Frank and Rutley until he retired. He maintained the keen interest in antiques and furniture that his auctioneering career had stimulated. Bill Clarke died on 4 April 1974.

B. T. COX

MANY miles from the sea in any direction, North Kilworth could nevertheless claim to have one Great War naval hero in Bernard Cox, son of the Rector. Cox was badly wounded in 1915 as he came under fire from Turkish shore batteries during an operation to clear a minefield in the Dardanelles. His courage earned him a DSO and Mention in Dispatches and his war service was followed by a successful career in the merchant fleet.

Bernard Thomas Cox found the pull of the sea greater than that of the ministry despite his father, grandfather and an elder brother being clergymen. His father, the Reverend Cecil Walker Cox, was the son of Thomas Cox, Rector of Kimcote, a couple of miles from North Kilworth, and it was at Kimcote that Cecil was born in 1844. Cecil was educated at Rugby and Magdalen College, Oxford, where he proved himself a fine cricketer and athlete. Ordained in 1868, he took over as Rector of Atherstone-on-Stour, a tiny village tucked away in the Warwickshire countryside south of Stratford-on-Avon, three years later. In 1878 he married London-born Louisa Bridges and the couple's six children were all born at the early Georgian rectory in Atherstone where a governess and three servants were employed. The couple's first child, Kenwrick, born in 1879, was followed by Eustace, Ursula, Bernard, Irene and Oliver. Eustace became a missionary in Rangoon, Burma, and later had his own parish in Norfolk.

Louisa died of cancer in November 1898. Whether Cecil thought a move would help him overcome his grief is not known but he became Rector of North Kilworth in 1901 when he was fifty-six. A lesser man might have found it daunting to be the first outsider appointed to a post held for two hundred years by the Belgrave family, still patrons of the living. But Mr Cox soon made his mark, with his sisters Jane and Alice taking on the mundane tasks and parish duties that normally fell to a minister's wife. The Rector's daughters were also able to play their part as they grew older. Cecil Cox's role meant he knew personally almost all of the village men who served in the Great War. When he helped officiate at the dedication of the war memorial in 1920 he could reflect with satisfaction that the familiar names freshly carved on the stone panels included those of Bernard and two of his other children, Irene and Oliver.

Bernard Cox, born on 22 June 1884, was sent to school at St Cuthbert's, Worksop. His maritime career started in the Mercantile Marine Training Ship Conway. He volunteered for the Royal Naval Reserve, made up of merchant navy officers, and was appointed midshipman in April 1903, rising to sub-lieutenant in 1911. He spent at least some leave at North Kilworth for he is recorded in 1908 as performing a humorous song at a musical evening there. The day after the outbreak of war he reported to the naval depot at Chatham and on 1 September 1914 he joined the Majestic Class battleship HMS Prince George as an acting lieutenant. PG, as the ship was nicknamed, was among

British and French warships due to launch an attack through the Dardanelles in March 1915, with a view to forcing a way into the Sea of Marmara and perhaps persuading Germany's ally Turkey to give up the fight. The naval attack failed, as did the landings on the Gallipoli peninsula that followed in April. However on the night of 13-14 March success still seemed within the Allies' grasp. An officer from Prince George was needed to take charge of trawler No 318 to sweep a minefield lying within range of the Turkish land batteries. (Thirty-five British and French trawlers had been converted into minesweepers for the Dardanelles operation.) Cox volunteered and, with a few men, started out accompanied by a sweeper. Cox's vessel ran the length of the minefield unmolested but just as it reached its turning point the Turks spotted it and opened up with a murderous fire from the shore. The trawler's fittings were torn away and most of her small crew became casualties. Cox was struck in the left elbow by shrapnel but refused to leave the bridge throughout the night despite having to hold his arm above his head to reduce the flow of blood from the wound. He finally piloted the battered trawler towards safety and a British destroyer came to the rescue. Cox was taken in the SS Plassy to the Royal Naval Hospital on Malta. He gained a mention in the Vice Admiral's dispatches and Cox's records praised him as 'a keen, gallant and trustworthy officer'.

By August 1915 Cox was recovering slowly after several operations and that month his appointment as Companion of the Distinguished Service Order was listed in *The London Gazette*. He was invested with the DSO on 9 September while in hospital at Plymouth. He was well enough the following month to marry Kathleen Audrey Couchman, second daughter of the Reverend Charles Couchman, Rector of Thornby, a Northamptonshire village about seven miles from Kilworth. Bernard's brother Oliver was best man. Soldiers sent from Northampton formed an archway of swords as the couple emerged from Thornby church and the bells rang there and at Kilworth. Those flourishes aside, the occasion was celebrated as an unostentatious 'war wedding'. The bride married in her travelling dress of navy blue and the numerous presents were not put on display.

Cox returned to service but was not in action again. He was demobilised in 1919 and two years later retired from the RNR as a lieutenant commander. By then he had resumed his career in the merchant navy and was on the China run as chief officer of the SS Telamon, owned by Alfred Holt & Co of

Liverpool. However, he and his wife maintained links with North Kilworth. Kathleen gave a violin solo at an entertainment for the upkeep of the Belgrave Memorial Hall in November 1924 and was involved in a Women's Institute event there in 1926. By the end of Cox's career in 1934 he was a captain of the Silver Line, commanding ships such as Silverpalm on voyages to Cape Town. He and his wife were living at Locking, near Weston-super-Mare in Somerset, when he died on 30 October 1935, aged fifty-one.

I. F. COX

ONE woman is named on North Kilworth's memorial. However, the nature of the war service that earned Irene Cox that distinction remains a puzzle. When the fete for the village's ex-servicemen was held in August 1919 a group of them posed for a photograph. Sitting in the middle of the front row, prominent between officers George Ball and Bill Clarke, was Miss Cox, the Rector's younger daughter. And, while each man received a silver matchbox honouring their war service, Irene Cox was presented with an engraved silver-topped toilet bottle. Newspaper reports of the event said the fete was in honour of the soldiers, sailors and *nurses* who had served in the war. However, no record appears of Miss Cox serving as a VAD (Voluntary Aid Detachment nurse) or in the First Aid Nursing Yeomanry. Perhaps she worked with the sick and wounded in a less formal fashion as did Kathleen Couchman, another clergyman's daughter who married Irene's brother Bernard and regularly visited the war hospital set up at Cottesbrooke, Northamptonshire. A story handed down in North Kilworth about Miss Cox 'driving officers in France' should be treated with caution. In 1922 Irene Cox was reported as attending a funeral as representative of the North and South Kilworth and Kimcote and Walton Nursing Association.

Irene Florence Cox was born at Atherstone-on-Stour in 1887 and baptised there by her father, the Reverend Cecil Cox, on 13 February that year *(see previous entry)*. Irene, only eleven when her mother died, was sent to boarding school in Kenilworth. She was fourteen when her father became Rector at North Kilworth but as she got older she became increasingly involved in church and village events. She was always on hand to help with

Rector's daughter Irene Cox (centre, fourth from left) with hockey and cricket players at North Kilworth after the war

treats for the Sunday school or church workers. Blessed with a fine soprano voice, Irene was in demand for fund-raising musical evenings at the Belgrave Memorial Hall. She was still greatly involved in village activities during the earlier part of the war at least.

In the 1920s, Miss Cox was secretary of the memorial hall committee, a member of the parochial church council, founder member of the Women's Institute, helper in the Girls Friendly Society, secretary and captain of the ladies' hockey club and driving force in the tennis club. Her links to the Great War are evident in the fact that she was chosen to place the ex-servicemen's wreath on the memorial at the Armistice Day ceremony in 1923.

And always there was the singing. There were few village entertainments that did not feature Miss Cox's solos or duets. She loved dressing up to appear in sketches with titles such as *Humphrey Hotspear Highwayman* or *The Jacobite*. She was a member of the church choir, performing solos at such events as harvest thanksgiving, and sometimes coached the schoolchildren. She was talented enough to win second place singing solo in a choir contest in Leicester in 1926. However, the following year the voice of Irene Cox was lost to North Kilworth when her father retired after fifty-nine years in holy orders. There were gifts and elaborate farewells to the Rector and his sisters Jane and Alice in May 1927. Irene was presented with a silver-mounted toilet set jointly by the choir and the hockey and tennis clubs. The Rector and Irene moved to Leamington Spa. Irene, who never married, became an active member of St John's church where her funeral service was held after she died in Leamington on 26 November 1966. She was seventy-nine.

O. B. COX

ONE son of North Kilworth's Rector was an early enthusiast for cars and motorcycles and his mechanical knowledge was to prove valuable to a wartime army which, although still hugely reliant on horses, was making increasing use of the internal combustion engine.

Oliver Bridges Cox – Bridges was his mother's maiden name – was the youngest of the Reverend Cecil Cox's six children *(see previous two entries)*. He was born at Atherstone-on-Stour on 25 November 1888 and baptised there by his father on 13 January 1889. Oliver, whose mother died a few days before his tenth birthday, was a boarder at St John's Foundation School in Leatherhead, Surrey. He became fascinated by motors and after studying at a technical college in Nottingham for two years he was apprenticed to the Rex Motor Company of Coventry. In 1908 he was mentioned in the local press for contributing two humorous songs and some conjuring tricks at a musical evening in North Kilworth where his sister Irene also sang. Cox spent six months in garage work in Rangoon, probably at the time that his eldest brother Eustace was a missionary there. He then had five years running and selling Thorneycroft lorries in Java and also knew Sumatra and Singapore. At some stage he returned to North Kilworth and he was twenty-four when he enlisted in the Army Service Corps at Rugby on 25 February 1916. Oliver became Private M2/156239 and rapidly proved himself thoroughly efficient and reliable in motor transport duties. The army had twigged that Cox was officer material and he was granted a temporary commission as a second lieutenant on 3 April. He was sent to the ASC depot at Bulford, Wiltshire, where he was attached to the 113th Siege Battery Royal Garrison Artillery, and remained with the Battery when it was sent to France on 13 June 1916. In February the following year he was at Deniécourt on the Somme when his left leg was grazed by a shell splinter. Cox, who had had varicose veins removed from both legs in 1915, was troubled by the wound, which became ulcerated and threatened to flare up if he walked too much. He was invalided home on 1 May 1917, was rated fit for home service only and had hospital treatment but that did not prevent him being promoted lieutenant that October. On 10 April 1918 he was posted to 977 Motor Transport Company at Norwich and was promoted acting captain to take command of the workshops there.

Cox was later judged fit to go abroad again with an MT Company and sailed for Mesopotamia from Southampton on 26 September 1918. (British and Indian forces had landed in Mesopotamia, now Iraq, in November 1914 to attack Germany's Turkish allies there. Good progress was made at first but in April 1916 thousands of British and Indian troops besieged at Kut surrendered and many died on the march into captivity. Britain regained the upper hand in 1917.) Cox arrived in Basra, after a stopover in Bombay, on 6 November 1918 by which time Turkey had surrendered. However, the old leg trouble returned and Cox was sent home. He finally left the army on 13 April 1920 with the rank of captain. He may have returned to Java for a while before going back to Kilworth. In later years he gave his address as that of his retired father in Leamington Spa. Further details of his life are not known.

G. C. CURRY

MANY of North Kilworth's servicemen had been taught at North Kilworth's school in Church Street during the regime of headmistress Fanny Curry. Her own boy was among them. George Charles Curry was the son of Fanny and her husband Herbert. Fanny was widowed with four children when she married Herbert, then a gamekeeper, in his home village of Foulden, Norfolk. The couple moved to Kilworth for Fanny to take over at the school on 30 March 1891. Her daughter Nellie Butters, aged fourteen, became monitor for the infants. George was born at North Kilworth on 25 June 1891 and baptised on 20 September.

George Curry in the uniform of the Royal Naval Air Service

As Fanny continued at the school her husband took on various jobs including gardening and acting as an agent for Prudential insurance. George started as a pupil on 21 June 1895. He was always something of an entertainer and took part in the comic sketch *Matrimonee* at a children's concert in April 1904. Perhaps it was an enthusiasm for performing that led George, at the age of sixteen, to temporarily forsake his trade as a fitter to join the Royal Marines as a band boy. He enlisted at Eastney, near Portsmouth, on 7 April 1908 and was given the service number 15832. He stayed in the

George Curry with his mother and sister Ethel at school pageant

Marines for only a little over fourteen months, time enough to have a Royal Marines crest tattooed on his right arm and an anchor on his left. Back in Kilworth he worked as a mechanic and was a keen cyclist, winning five shillings (25p) at the 1910 flower show sports for gaining second place in the gents' comic costume bike race.

George's mechanical skills were to make him useful to the rapidly expanding air forces after war came. He joined the Royal Naval Air Service on 24 February 1916 as an air mechanic and worked on aero engines. Curry appears to have been based in Britain until 14 April 1917 when he was posted to Otranto in Italy. He was still there on 1 April 1918 when the RNAS and Royal Flying Corps became the Royal Air Force and his rank was changed to corporal mechanic. He was promoted sergeant mechanic that August and was posted home in April 1919 to be put on the RAF reserve.

War service over, Curry went back to being a motor mechanic but also operated a 30cwt Ford lorry to deliver goods to and from Welford and Kilworth station. On summer weekends he sometimes rigged up seats on the rear of the vehicle to run outings under the banner of Bluebird Coaches. Bluebird was also the name given to the dance band which he ran in the mid-1920s and which belted out numbers such as *Rendezvous* and *Swanee River* at concerts and charity events. George, on the piccolo, was joined by Gwendoline Scobie on piano, Alf Pitcher on violin and former soldier Arthur Whyles on cornet. On June 27 1925 George married one of George Ball's daughters, Jessie. The couple had three daughters, although one died in infancy. They moved to Dunchurch, near Rugby, when George became manager of a garage for local firm Sam Robbins. During the Second World War he was chief of the auxiliary fire service section in Dunchurch. George continued in the motor trade and acted as mechanic for a pal who raced on the Isle of Man. He also took pride in keeping an immaculate garden and liked to go fishing. George Curry was sixty-eight when he died on 27 December 1959.

F. M. DILKS

FRED Dilks was a son of the stationmaster at Welford and Kilworth station. His father, also Frederick, had worked for the railway for many years. Originally from Watford, Hertfordshire, Frederick senior was employed at Thorpe station, near Thrapston in Northamptonshire, before he and his wife Sarah moved to North Kilworth in the 1880s. Welford and Kilworth was busy for a country station and an idea of the staffing levels can be gained from the fact that there were twenty diners when Dilks laid on an employees' treat at the Swan Inn in 1903.

Frederick and Sarah had three sons. Frederick Mayes Dilks, the youngest, was born at Kilworth on 15 January 1896. Little has emerged about Fred's war service. One clue comes from a letter he sent to his great pal Victor Ball *(see V. E. Ball, The Fallen)* in 1918. The note was dated 24 August from Bombay and invited a reply to Naval House, Port Said.

Fred, who worked as an electrical engineer, married but had no children. At some stage he lived in east London and later Barrow-in-Furness but always kept in touch with old friends in North Kilworth, including the Balls and Ernie Spiers. Fred Dilks was eighty-three when he died at Barrow on 9 February 1979.

T. H. DILKS

THE demands of wartime saw Thomas Dilks become a stationmaster like his father Frederick. However, while Frederick was employed by the London and North Western Railway Company, his son was a soldier in the Royal Engineers when it operated railways in Mesopotamia.

Thomas Harry Dilks was Frederick's eldest son and is named on North Kilworth war memorial with his brother Fred *(see previous entry)*. Another boy John, born between Thomas and Fred, may not have served in the war. Thomas was born in August 1884 at Thorpe Apechurch, Northamptonshire, when his father worked at the local station. Frederick seems to have been appointed stationmaster at Welford and Kilworth soon afterwards as Thomas was baptised at nearby Husbands Bosworth on 15 October 1884.

After school days Thomas followed his father into railway employment, becoming a goods clerk. However he was a commercial traveller by the time he married on 20 April 1912 at the age of twenty-seven. His bride was Winifred Carter, a twenty-four-year-old dressmaker from Little Bowden, near Market Harborough, and the ceremony was held at Little Bowden parish church. The couple went to live in Nithsdale Avenue, Market Harborough, and their son Thomas Arthur was born in June the following year.

Dilks was thirty-one when he enlisted under the Derby Scheme on 30 November 1915. It meant that he went on to the army reserve until his services were needed and he eventually joined for duty at Weedon in Northamptonshire on 6 June 1916, becoming Gunner 152949 in the Royal Field Artillery. He was later posted to 47th (Reserve) Battery and was promoted bombardier (corporal) on 8 December 1916. In 1917 he was sent to join the expeditionary force fighting the Turks in Mesopotamia (now Iraq) and embarked at Devonport on 25 September. Perhaps as a consequence of his civilian railway experience, Dilks was transferred to the Royal Engineers on 12 February 1918 and posted to join railway troops in Mesopotamia as a 'superior stationmaster'. He became Sapper 346813. Dilks had two brief stays in hospital, in Basra and Makina, for unspecified complaints during his time in Mesopotamia but performed his duties well. By the time he was posted home early in 1919 he was Acting Sergeant WR/298342. Details of Thomas Dilks's later life are not known.

Fred Dilks pictured in later life   **David Dorman in Yeomanry**

D. I. DORMAN

THE youngest of the three Dorman brothers who became soldiers in the Great War was David, who was only eighteen at the time of the Armistice. He was born in 1900, the son of William and Sarah Jane Dorman, and baptised David Isaac at St Andrew's, North Kilworth, on 22 April that year. He started at the village school on 13 March 1903, the same day as Henry Pebody, another future soldier, and passed his exam to leave in July 1912. David was fifteen when his eldest brother John died in France *(see J. Dorman, The Fallen)*. Towards the end of the war he joined the Staffordshire Yeomanry but it is not known where he served. He married Grace Peabody in her home village of South Kilworth in June 1922. The couple, who were to have three sons, made their home in the village. David worked for a timber firm at the time of his marriage but later took a job in the foundry at engineering firm Willans in Rugby. During the Second World War he was granted a petrol allowance for his motorcycle to enable him to do shift work there. He was also a member of the Home Guard. David Dorman died in November 1952 aged fifty-two.

J. DORMAN

JOE Dorman joined his brother David *(see previous entry)* at the North Kilworth fete honouring the village's servicemen in August 1919. Both men were in uniform for the occasion. While enjoying the festive atmosphere they must have paused to remember their brother John whose name would join those of Kilworth's other war dead on the village memorial. Joseph Henry Dorman, son of William and Sarah Jane Dorman, was born in 1889 and baptised at Kilworth on 22 December that year. He started at the village school on 9 June 1893 as an infant and was twelve when, on 3 March 1902, he passed the exam for his labour certificate. Joe was in the army during the Great War. Details of his service have not surfaced but his sergeant's stripes are clear in a photograph of the 1919 fete. After the war he returned to his parents on the Rugby Road in North Kilworth for a while. He later married, had a son and daughter, and lived in Rugby where he worked as a driver for Sam Robbins, the removals firm.

C. W. DUNKLEY

VILLAGERS like Charlie Dunkley were the lifeblood of the community. He was a member of North Kilworth's football team, brass band and air rifle club, a church sidesman, chorister and, in later years, secretary of the Oddfellows' lodge and vice-chairman of the ex-servicemen's club. In a highly skilled job and married with two young daughters when war came, he could have been excused for allowing younger men to fill the gaps in the army's ranks until conscription loomed. That was not Charlie Dunkley's way; by early 1915 he was serving his country as a volunteer soldier and continued to do so for the next four years.

He was born on 28 December 1884, the only child of Joseph Dunkley and his wife Hannah, née Pebody, who had married at North Kilworth in 1879. When the couple registered their son's birth they gave his name as Charles William Crow Dunkley. Joseph's second name was also Crow, a token of the Dunkleys having married, in a previous generation, into the Crow family, also of North Kilworth. There is no indication that Charles ever used the name and, indeed, it was not included in the baptism register when Rector Belgrave christened him in February 1885.

Charles, whose parents lived in Station Road, started at North Kilworth school in June 1888 before he was four. He left on 26 May 1897 and at some stage started work at Ball's, where his father was a blacksmith's striker. For a while Charles was given the task of painting the implements produced by the firm but then served his five-year apprenticeship as a wheelwright. Young Dunkley was also something of an entertainer. In 1901 he played the part of Mrs Stout in an entertainment called *The Magic Horn* staged in the schoolroom by the Boys' Bible Class. He played the cornet in the village band and joined the handbell ringers who toured Kilworth each Christmas. Charles could also be relied on to provide a song during musical evenings at the Belgrave Memorial Hall. He was keen on sport and did well in the races at the annual flower show. He was good enough at football to be given a trial at Leicester Fosse (forerunner of Leicester City) but nothing came of it. Charles was in his early twenties when he was a member of the air rifle club that had moderate success locally.

On 9 September 1910 Charles married Lincolnshire-born Lily Parratt, then a domestic servant at Knighton Hall, near Leicester. The couple were both twenty-five at the time of their wedding at St Andrew's, where Charles's young workmate, Bert Cheney, was one of the witnesses. Charles and Lily made their home at Western Cottages, built for Ball's workers. The couple's first child Dorothy was born on Boxing Day 1911 and their second, Marjorie, was born on 11 September 1913. The *Rugby Advertiser* recorded in December 1914 that six married men from North Kilworth, including Charles Dunkley, Arthur Whyles and George Morris, had offered to serve in the

Royal Army Medical Corps. Whatever the accuracy of the report, none of those men ended up as army medics and it was Dunkley's skills as a wheelwright that would be valuable to the army. Records show that Charles passed a medical at Lutterworth on 19 December. At the same time George Ball was asked to provide a reference in which he confirmed that he had known Dunkley for many years, that he was employed by him as a wheelwright and 'body maker general' and that he was useful, honest and sober with 'nothing against him' regarding character. Charles enlisted at Glen Parva barracks, Leicester, on 23 December. However he was not summoned for service immediately. He and Arthur Whyles were among those who provided the musical entertainment for the annual memorial hall social and dance in January 1915. Charles reported back to Glen Parva on 1 March and was sent immediately to the Army Service Corps in Aldershot where he became Wheeler T/4 065387. He soon passed his skills test in the workshops and was promoted corporal in April. He was posted from 45th Reserve Park to 120 Company and later to No 2 Depot at Woolwich. By December 1917 Dunkley was back at Aldershot where he wrote home from 580 Company ASC at Buller Barracks to thank Kilworth's parishioners for their Christmas parcel. 'The pie and cake will make a very nice change from army mess room menu,' he said. Charles added, 'It is a great pleasure to us to know the people at home don't forget us, this is my third Xmas away from home and I hope it will be the last.'

Tragedy struck the Dunkley family the following month. Lily sent a note into school on 28 January 1918 excusing six-year-old Dorothy's absence because of a sore throat. The child died two days later, a victim of diphtheria. (The Dunkleys would have a third daughter Sheila in March 1920. She and Marjorie both won scholarships to Lutterworth Grammar School.) Charles was demobbed on 9 May 1919 and returned to work at Ball's. But he was among the men laid off as the firm felt the effects of the Depression and increased use of cheap, machine-made wheels. Six months out of work was a distressing experience for a man to whom duty to employer and community were second nature. Charles wrote in response to an advert in the *Daily Chronicle* for skilled artificers for the army reserve. His war experience and civilian skills were not enough to gain him a position. He took to cycling many miles to take work as a carpenter on building sites. Later employment on building works at Rugby School at least meant he could take the train

Corporal Charles Dunkley (centre) was one of several Kilworth men who found themselves in the Army Service Corps. The skills of George Ball's wheelwrights, in particular, were invaluable to a corps responsible for the transport of the army's vital supplies from Kilworth. Concern over work did not stop Charles playing his part in village life and 1925 found him acting as MC at a whist drive to raise cash for repairs to the church spire.

For several years Charles had the important role of secretary to the village's Oddfellows Lodge, which met in the schoolroom. In 1930 he administered lodge business for forty-two members and for fifty-five by 1940, overseeing the collection of contributions on lodge nights. During the Second World War Charles was an air raid warden and the old soldier could take pride in his daughter Sheila serving in the ATS (Auxiliary Territorial Service, the women's army). For about the last twelve years of his life he worked as a maintenance carpenter at British Thomson-Houston (BTH) in Rugby. Charles Dunkley died, aged sixty-one, on 31 August 1946. Lily died in 1963. In November 1964, the couple's daughters honoured their memory by presenting St Andrew's with bookshelves that are still in use.

B. GUDGER

W HEN Ben Gudger wed his long-time sweetheart he had no inkling that his married life would be disrupted by army service. The Great War was still five years away and Ben's thoughts were concentrated on working hard to provide for his new wife and any children that were to come along. However, like so many other of North Kilworth's men, he was to find himself in the uniform of the Army Service Corps, although for only a relatively brief period.

Benjamin Gudger was born in Welford on 23 January 1882, son of Meshack Gudger, a farm labourer, and his wife Susannah. He is thought to have had two sisters and two brothers. For several years Ben courted Alice Willson, meaning a bicycle ride of twelve fairly hilly miles each way to Wigston Magna, where she lived. Alice, who worked in a local shoe factory, was one of four children of a widowed mother, and therefore understood the importance of thrift, a useful quality in a bride. Ben, a coal carter, was twenty-seven and Alice twenty-five when they married at All Saints, Wigston, on 31 July 1909. The couple at first lived in Welford but later moved to a cottage in Station Road, North Kilworth, which was handier for that village's coal yard. Their son Benjamin John was born in 1914.

Ben Gudger, his coal deliveries completed, pauses for the camera on his way back to the yard

Ben and Alice Gudger with family at their wedding in July 1909

Ben was thirty-four with a wife expecting their second child when he went to Rugby to enlist in the army on 12 May 1916. The couple's daughter Alice was born in the August. Ben had still not been summoned for duty when Alice died, aged only nineteen months, on 22 March 1918. But on 22 July of that year he reported for duty at Glen Parva barracks. He became Private M/413732 Gudger in 12 Company Army Service Corps and served at depots including Osterley Park, Middlesex, on mechanical transport duties. One benefit of being in the army was that he was taught to drive lorries. On 25 October 1918 he was admitted to hospital with influenza. His robust constitution doubtless helped him survive a pandemic which killed so many others but it was some weeks before he was fit to return to duty. Ben was demobbed in February 1919, rated as intelligent, reliable and sober.

He returned to Kilworth where, in 1922, he and Alice had a second son, Eric Willson Gudger. In about 1925 the family moved to Kimberley Road, Rugby. Ben worked for many years at Ellis and Everard, who ran a coal and animal feed business at the railway goods yards in nearby Wood Street. On his retirement Ben was presented with a clock but he was such a valued employee that he was immediately coaxed back by the bosses and remained with the firm into his seventies. He is fondly remembered as a popular, hard-working man with a mischievous but never malicious sense of humour. One of his favourite stories from his days as a coal carter was the way he had to put a sack over his horse's head as the only way of persuading the animal to pull its load up the long drag of John Ball Hill on the Leicester-to-Welford road.

Ben and Alice celebrated their golden wedding in 1959. They were still living in Kimberley Road when Ben died on 1 February 1962 aged eighty. Alice died four years later.

Ben Gudger in Service Corps

A. W. I. HANCOCK

TWO Hancock brothers went to war and the younger, Billy, was another of the Kilworth men to join the Army Service Corps. Albert Willy Isaac Hancock was born on 23 March 1899, the son of Leonard and Rebecca Hancock, who lived in Walton, a village to the north of Kilworth. Leonard was a labourer at the time but later worked as a wagoner. Little has emerged about Billy's early life but during the war he joined the ASC as a driver on horse transport and was given the army number T/382652. He served abroad but does not seem to have entered any war zone before 1916. After demob he lived in Church Street, North Kilworth.

G. L. HANCOCK

THE elder Hancock brother, George, was a husband and father when the army sent him to France. He served there in two of Britain's most renowned infantry regiments before he returned to civilian life.

George Leonard Hancock was born at Walton on 10 September 1893. He was given a third name Cave, his mother's maiden name, but never used it. Like his father, George was a wagoner. He was living in North Kilworth when on 14 December 1915 he married Kate Wearing, the nineteen-year-old daughter of a Kilworth family. She had worked as a domestic servant in various households since leaving school at twelve. The couple wed at St Andrew's where both had been confirmed. Three months after the ceremony George was called up. He presented himself at Leicester on 14 March 1916 and was posted to the Durham Light Infantry. As Private 301208 the twenty-two-year-old recruit was sent to the 5th Reserve Battalion and spent the rest of the year in England, during which time his first son Ronald was born. However, Hancock was sent to France on 4 January 1917 and there is no record of him returning home until he was granted fourteen days' leave in January 1918. During the wholesale reorganisation of units in 1918 Hancock was transferred on 17 August to the 6th (Service) Battalion of The Buffs (East Kent Regiment) and given the new regimental number 14906. Posted to B Company, he stayed in France and on the day of the Armistice he was with his unit, part of the 37th Brigade 12th Division, at Rumegies, a village near the Belgian border south east of Lille. George was sent home on fourteen days' leave on 2 January 1919 and that was extended until the following month when his demob came through.

After the war George worked with horses for farmer Tom Whiteman and his duties included fetching timber from Stanford Park. It is said his wages were 17s 6d (87p) a week. He later took on contract work. He helped to form the village's ex-servicemen's club, supported the local football side and was a founder member of a local National Union of Agricultural Workers branch. During the 1920s he helped with the sideshows at the annual flower show, running table skittles, and managing on one occasion to win a prize for his onions. He and Kate had four more sons and two daughters. In the Second World War George was in the Home Guard while eldest son Ron rose to be a sergeant in the Coldstream Guards. Ron, wounded by a sniper while in charge of a tank in 1945, was chairman of the Husbands Bosworth branch of the British Legion in the 1960s. George and Kate, who lived at 1 Council Houses, were members of Kilworth's Evergreen Club by the time they celebrated their golden wedding at a family party in December 1965. George died on 3 March 1969 aged seventy-five. At the funeral at St Andrew's his coffin was draped with the Union Flag as was his due.

George Hancock with his wife Kate and their son Ronald in 1916

P. J. HAYNES

FARMER'S son Percy Haynes, one of the younger men named on Kilworth's memorial, was in the army for only about the last twelve months of the war but it was long enough for him to see some serious action. Percy James Haynes was born in August 1898. His father James, originally from Rothwell in Northamptonshire, farmed on Pincet Lane, the road to Leicester from Kilworth. James and his wife Susan had their son baptised at St Andrew's on 9 October. Percy's brother Gordon was a couple of years older but diphtheria had left him unfit for army service. Another brother Watson was three years younger than Percy and so not of an age to serve. (There were also two sisters.) Percy's army records have not survived but at some stage he ceased working on his father's farm to become Private 76457 in the Manchester Regiment. This was the regiment of Wilfred Owen, one of the greatest of war poets, who was killed a week before the Armistice in November 1918.

According to one story Percy related in later years he was lucky to have survived the war. He told how he and a fellow farmer-turned-soldier were late returning to camp ready for embarkation with their unit. The story goes that by the time the pair caught up with their comrades in France many had already been wiped out in action. Percy also told how he was caught by machine-gun fire during a night patrol. He escaped despite one bullet denting his helmet and another going through his trouser leg. Percy was also close by when an officer was killed as a shell splintered an ash tree. On a lighter note, Percy regularly won when pals in their bell tent put up a penny a head, with the cash going to the man who told the best joke.

Percy returned to farming after the war and was keen on motorcycles. But the daredevil trait failed to impress his father when Percy and brother Gordon smashed James's car into a gate after failing to straighten up after a corner. In 1925 Percy married Mary Ball, of Claybrooke Magna. They farmed at Ashby Parva where they kept dairy cows and made Leicestershire cheese, winning cups at agricultural shows. Percy Haynes was seventy-one when he died in August 1969.

Percy Haynes aged 19 in 1917 shortly before he went off to war

T. P. HILL

AS other stories from the memorial show, young single men ready for adventure had no monopoly when it came to serving in the Great War. Percy Hill was another example of a settled husband and father who donned uniform in his thirties to serve his country. He was born at North Kilworth on 7 February 1884, the son of William Hill, a grazier and sometime ale and porter dealer, and his wife Frances, both natives of the village. Percy and his brother Edwin, a year older, were baptised together at St Andrew's by Rector Belgrave on 4 May 1884. Percy, christened Thomas Percy but always known by his second name, started at the village school when he was four. Before the war he worked as a general helper before becoming a painter at Ball's where Edwin was a wheelwright and carpenter. Evidence of Percy's lifelong interest in gardening appeared as early as 1904 when his carrots earned him a place in one of the vegetable classes at Kilworth's sixth annual horticultural show. He also played for the village football team and was a member of the air rifle club. In 1905 he married Welsh girl Hannah Griffiths in her home area of Denbighshire. (Hannah was in service for the Entwisles at Kilworth House for many years. Her diligence as lady's maid was recognised when widowed Florence Entwisle left her £100 in her will in 1953.) Percy and Hannah had a son Stanley in 1906 and a daughter Favell six years later.

It is uncertain when Percy joined the army but by the end of 1917 he was a gunner serving with 493 Siege Battery of the Royal Garrison Artillery at Lydd Camp, Kent. After the war he went back to work as a painter and acted as sidesman at St Andrew's, where his wife was also a willing helper. Percy Hill was only forty-seven when he died in November 1931. His daughter died the following June, aged twenty. Stanley Hill married Evelyn, sister of George Stock *(see G.W. Stock, The Fallen),* in 1935, thus uniting two of the families that had members named on the war memorial. Percy's widow Hannah, staunch member of the Women's Institute and Mothers' Union and remembered for her gentle nature, lived in High Street until her death in November 1967, aged eighty-six.

Percy Hill on a break from duties in the Royal Garrison Artillery

War veteran Percy Hill on lawn-mowing duty in his garden

J. HOWKINS

THE Howkins family dealt with the Royal Mail in North Kilworth when Queen Victoria was a young woman and was still doing so decades into the reign of her great-great-grand-daughter Elizabeth. James Howkins, whose father Stephen was the first family member to run the village's sub-post office, spent his working life dealing with the mail and telegrams that passed through there. His sterling service was interrupted only by his time in the army in the Great War, in which he was taken prisoner. The family came from Bitteswell, the other side of Lutterworth from Kilworth, where parish registers dating back to 1558 list them as shoemakers, tailors and bakers. Stephen, born in Bitteswell, moved to Kilworth where he set up business as a boot and shoemaker. In 1847 he started receiving the village's mail at a converted malthouse next to the White Lion. Letters arrived daily at Welford by coach and were then carried to Kilworth on horseback. Stephen combined the mail duties with his shoemaking, hiking to Leicester a couple of times a week to fetch leather.

James, youngest of Stephen and his wife Jane's nine children, was born on 5 October 1880 and baptised at St Andrew's on 17 June 1883. As a young man he worked for his father as a postman and telegraph clerk. James was twenty-two when he married Louisa Elizabeth Hobson, the twenty-one-year-old daughter of a shepherd from Elkington, near Welford. The ceremony was at Welford parish church on 22 July 1903. A couple of years previously James's father had finally retired as sub-postmaster at the age of seventy-nine. He was presented with a purse of money from grateful villagers as there was no post office pension. James's eldest sister Maria briefly took charge of the sub-post office but resigned in favour of James in 1903. By then the mail came from Rugby in a van drawn by two horses. With no telephone in the village the telegraph office was also kept fairly busy.

In his spare time James played for the village football team and the meticulous account-keeping required of a sub-postmaster made him the obvious choice to be treasurer and secretary of the club. He was father to two sons and two daughters by the time he enlisted in the army in June 1916. Details are scant but it is thought it was February 1918 when he was taken prisoner by the Germans. He was released at Christmas that year and was

James Howkins outside Kilworth's post office in the early 1900s

the last of Kilworth's prisoners of war to return home. James was discharged from the army in March 1919 and his third son was born later that year.

In the 1920s James played for the village cricket team and was secretary to the ex-servicemen's club, helping to organise its annual outing. He was also one of the veterans who took part in the annual cleaning and tidying of the war memorial on which his own name was inscribed. James continued as the village's diligent sub-postmaster although his health started to suffer, probably due in part to the poor conditions he endured as a prisoner. He died at his home on 23 May 1934, aged fifty-three. James's widow then ran the post office until the couple's eldest son Frank took over in 1953, by which time the business had moved to new premises a few yards away. The post office remained in the family after Frank, a former parish council chairman, died in 1973. The family's garage business, alongside the post office, has also been a feature of North Kilworth for many years.

F. KNIGHT

THE Knights, Frank and John, are another example of North Kilworth brothers who served in the Great War. They were among four sons of William Knight, who appears in records variously described as a shepherd, grazier and farm labourer. William and his wife Elizabeth also had a daughter Florence. Frank, the youngest child, was born on 19 September 1894 and baptised at St Andrew's on 9 June the following year. At the 1902 flower show sports at Kilworth House Frank won the fifty-yards race for boys under eight, beating George Ball and William Burbidge into second and third places respectively. One wonders whether those three, after they had returned from fighting for their country, ever recalled that day of innocent summer fun they had enjoyed together as lads. Frank started work labouring on a farm but later became a wheelwright, probably at Ball's. He was a member of North Kilworth's air rifle club.

Frank was twenty-one and unmarried when he went to Lutterworth to attest for the army on 11 December 1915. He was placed on the reserve and it was June 1916 before he was called to Weedon to join the Royal Field Artillery as Gunner 152955. By the end of the month Frank had passed the trade test as a wheeler and was posted to a reserve brigade. He remained in Britain until 9 July 1917 when he was sent out as part of the Egypt Expeditionary Force which was pushing the Turks across Sinai and into Palestine. Frank was not demobbed until December 1919 by which time he had been promoted wheeler corporal. He returned to North Kilworth and was twenty-six when, on 4 June 1921, he married Elizabeth May Ware, the twenty-eight-year-old daughter of a farm bailiff, at Holy Trinity Church, Rugby. The couple had two sons, Mervyn and Cyril, and at one stage the family lived in Kilworth with Frank's mother, who had been widowed in 1917.

Frank appears to have had some affinity with South Kilworth; certainly he turned out for that village's football team. Early in 1920 he helped his side to a three-one victory while playing centre-half in a home match against North Kilworth in the Harborough and District League. He 'proved himself a tower of strength and scored a fine goal', said a match report. But he remained loyal to North Kilworth in other respects. Frank was a member of the ex-servicemen's club and when about sixty former soldiers and friends had their annual supper at the Belgrave Memorial Hall in 1923 he was one of those applauded for giving a song to round off the evening. Two years later it was Frank, with Arthur Whyles and Ernie Spiers, who gave the war memorial its annual spruce-up, repainting the railings and names on the panels. He and his wife had left North Kilworth by 1928.

J. H. KNIGHT

JOHN Henry Knight was one of Frank's elder brothers *(see previous entry)* and was born at North Kilworth on 15 December 1885. He attended the village school but, for some reason, he left with the eldest brother Charles in June 1895 to go to South Kilworth school. (Another brother William and sister Florence were born between John and Frank.) Back in North Kilworth, John took the part of Humpty Dumpty in an entertainment staged in the schoolroom by the Boys' Bible Class in 1901. He was a sporting youngster, often making a good showing in the athletics at the annual flower show sports. He was also a keen cyclist, who won the mile-and-a-half race at the show in 1908, having come second in the event the previous two years.

It is not certain but John Knight is thought to have been a private in the Leicestershire Yeomanry who was later transferred to the Hussars and sent to Egypt in October 1915. After the war he is believed to have stayed briefly in North Kilworth but nothing of his later life has come to light.

G. W. LOOMES

THE majority of men who fought in the Great War did so in the army but even landlocked North Kilworth provided its share of sailors. Among them was George Loomes, who served in the Royal Marines as well as in the Royal Navy and was in uniform again in the Second World War as a police officer.

George Walter Loomes was born at Kilworth on 24 October 1899. His father Walter, who served in the Army Ordnance Corps at some stage, had married Elizabeth Affleck, a laundress and daughter of a military man, earlier

George Loomes as a young marine (left). He was later in the Royal Navy (above) and became a PC (below) in the Second World War

that year. The couple lived in London while their son stayed with Walter's parents in Kilworth. Walter's father William Charles Loomes, aged forty-four at the turn of the century, was known as Little Grandpap in the family and was a staunch chapelgoer. He lived with his wife Fanny in Little London off the South Kilworth road. (William and Fanny also had a daughter Ellen. She was working in a London hotel when she met and married Italian waiter Ernesto Bozzoni. The couple, who eventually had eight children, went to live in North Kilworth, where the Bozzoni name is still remembered.) George Loomes started at Kilworth school on 5 September 1904 and remained there until he passed the leaving exam in July 1912 at the same time as David Dorman *(see D. I. Dorman, this chapter)*.

He was working as a farm labourer and was still a couple of weeks shy of his eighteenth birthday when he went to Nottingham to enlist in the Royal Marines Artillery as Private 15953 on 10 October 1917. He stated his religion as Wesleyan and gave his mother's address as Southwark, south-east London. At 5ft 11in, George was a tall youth by the standards of the time. At Christmas 1917 he was in barracks in Portsmouth and was made gunner second class on 23 April 1918. On 17 July 1918 he was posted as a gunner in HMS Tiger, a sleek and speedy battlecruiser launched in 1912 and repaired after it was badly damaged in the Battle of Jutland in 1916. After the war ended Loomes received a £10 gratuity and small sums from Tiger's naval prize fund. In 1919 he volunteered for special service in the Royal Navy. He transferred to become a stoker first class on 23 April that year and served in the Tiger and other vessels including the Blake and Blenheim, ageing cruisers that had been converted into depot ships for destroyers. By the time George's service expired in 1922 he had married Florence Courteney, of Marylebone, London. He returned to civilian work but had been recommended for part-time service with the Royal Fleet Reserve with whom he remained until discharged in July 1928. His conduct had been rated consistently as very good throughout his time in uniform. He worked as a packer and fur sorter at Blatspiel Stamp and Heacock, long-established importers near Southwark Bridge in the City of London, until 1931 when the Depression forced the firm to close its operation. With a glowing reference, George found work at another, nearby fur and skin company, Spalding and Wickham Jones. In June 1934 he married his second wife Ivy Wilkes, by whom he had two daughters. The family lived in Mitcham, south-west London.

George's employers reluctantly let him go when, in 1939, he decided to join the Metropolitan Police as a full-time special constable. He started his duties the day Britain declared war, 3 September, and later became an officer at Wandsworth prison. After the war the pressure on firms to export ensured that George found work back in his former trade on his old riverside patch. Brooks Wharf and Bull Wharf Ltd, of Upper Thames Street, took him on sorting the large quantities of Russian furs they were handling for the export trade.

Although his working life was spent in London, George never forgot the Leicestershire village where he was brought up and his house in Mitcham was named Kilworth. A reminder of his links to the village came in 1946 when he acted as sole executor on the death of grandad Loomes at the age of ninety. That chapel stalwart was recalled by older residents as a small, white-bearded figure who swept the village roads and spent much of his time in the tin hut in his garden. George Loomes is remembered as a man of dry wit who was very strict though fair with his daughters. He died aged seventy-seven on 22 December 1976.

F. C. MORLEY

THE Morley brothers, Walter and Frank, were born in North Kilworth two years apart. Both attended the village school and played football for Kilworth, both worked for Ball's and both were married men and fathers before the outbreak of war. And both Morleys became soldiers, returning home after the end of hostilities to resume family life. Walter and Frank were the sons of David Right Morley, originally from Clipston in Northamptonshire, and his Kilworth-born wife Mary. The couple lived in Church Street. David, an agricultural labourer who kept one of the best allotments in the village, later earned the description grazier and eventually farmer. It is purely speculation but perhaps David, said to be an expert in land drainage, earned enough to buy land in his own right. Certainly he and Mary were able to move to a house and plot at Highwayside, on the west side of the road to South Kilworth. During the war the couple endured the worry of having not only two sons serving abroad but also a son-in-law. Elsie Minnie, the youngest of their three daughters and a dressmaker, married soldier Horace Sharp soon after war was declared. Horace *(see H. Sharp, this chapter)* was wounded and captured but returned home safely.

Francis Cave Morley, younger of the Morley brothers, was born on 2 August 1887. He started at the village school on 6 November 1891. It is not recorded when he left but he became a blacksmith and farrier for Ball's. As a youth he was a keen member of the air rifle club and, with his brother, competed in the cycle races at the annual flower show. Frank was twenty-four when he married sixteen-year-old Sarah Atkins at her local parish church in Walsgrave-on-Sowe, Coventry, on 23 March 1912. The bride's late father had been a miner. The couple's first son, Francis Alex David, was born later that year. A second son, Thomas Walter, was born on 4 October 1914. It seems the couple lived initially at Walsgrave but had both of their sons baptised at Kilworth. Thomas was taken to the font on 4 April 1915 only a few weeks before his father was sent overseas by the army. Frank had attested at Coventry and joined the Army Service Corps as Driver TS/6017 at 2 Depot Company, Woolwich, on 21 February. He was appointed a shoeing smith and remained in Britain until 14 April 1915 when he was sent to join the Egypt Expeditionary Force. There are no details of his service abroad and he was demobilised in February 1919. Frank appears to have returned to Kilworth but at some stage took his family to live in Walsgrave, where he later kept a general store. He died aged sixty-nine at Coventry on 7 December 1956.

W. J. MORLEY

THE elder Morley brother, Walter, was among the first village men to leave for war. He was born on 16 June 1885 and called Walter John Bennett, the last of those christian names being his mother's maiden name *(see previous entry)*. Like his brother Frank and sisters, he attended the village school and was granted his labour certificate in July 1896. Walter at first worked in farming like his father but was later taken on at Ball's to train as a wheelwright.

He played for Kilworth's football team alongside Frank and other future soldiers, such as Charlie Dunkley and Jim Howkins, and also competed in the athletics and cycle racing at the flower show sports. On 1 July 1907 he married Agnes Muggleton at the parish church in the east Leicestershire village of Hallaton where she was then living. Agnes, aged twenty-two like her husband, was born in Preston, Rutland, daughter of coachman Harry

Frank Morley, one of Kilworth's married men who joined up

Frank Morley with his wife Sarah. The couple married in 1912

Muggleton. Walter took his bride back to North Kilworth to live and their first son Walter Thomas Harry was baptised there on 14 February 1909. In 1913 Walter, like his workmates George Ball Jnr and Ted Cheney, joined the Leicestershire Yeomanry as a private. His regimental number 1946 was one previous to Cheney's. Walter and his chums were mobilised on the outbreak of war and he, Ball and Cheney landed in France together on 2 November 1914. The Yeomanry's exploits in cavalry and infantry roles, at Ypres and elsewhere, are detailed in the entry on George Ball. However, Morley's service differed from that of his friends after the Yeomanry underwent a wholesale shake-up later in the war. Records show he spent time with the Royal Flying Corps in some unspecified capacity before moving on to a Hussars unit. It is uncertain whether he returned to Ball's when peace came. He later moved to Coventry, possibly influenced by his brother Frank living there, and worked as a carpenter. For a while after the German blitz on Coventry in November 1940 Walter took his family to live with his sister Elsie and brother-in-law Horace, who had taken over the Morley parents' home on the South Kilworth road. Walter Morley died on 17 November 1959.

Walter Morley with his wife Agnes whom he married in 1907

G. H. MORRIS

BLACKSMITH William Morris and his wife Eliza were among the parents who endured the anxiety of having two sons in uniform. George and Tom were themselves both fathers by the time they went to war. The elder of the brothers, George, completed his service unscathed but Tom was seriously wounded, although that did not prevent him from returning to the front or going back to work after his eventual discharge. Between George and Tom was another son Bob, who did not serve. The brothers' father, originally from the Leicestershire village of Ashby Magna, was for many years one of Ball's leading workmen and noted for the excellence of the ironwork he produced for carts. He also served as parish constable at some stage. Eliza, née Dickins, was from Boughton, Northamptonshire. The couple lived with their family – there was also a daughter, Amy – in the first of Western Cottages, closest to Ball's, on the Lutterworth Road. Eliza never saw her boys return from the war; she died aged sixty-five on 1 November 1916 after months of illness.

George Herbert Morris was born on 5 November 1880 and baptised on 13 February 1881. He attended the village school but in 1894 he and his three siblings were absent for two months with fever. They returned to lessons in the November. After school George followed his father's example by working for Ball's, serving a five-year apprenticeship as a wheelwright. George was a keen sportsman, particularly when it came to football. He was playing for North Kilworth away to Market Harborough Excelsior in March 1906 when, three minutes after kick-off, he slipped and broke a leg. A doctor set the limb and George was carried home in an ambulance wagon, leaving his team-mates to lose 7-0. George also shot for the village's air rifle club and was elected on to its committee in 1909. He was a keen cyclist and competed in the flower show sports. At the 1910 event he won a ten-shilling (50p) prize by coming first in the gents' comic costume cycle parade in the guise of a suffragette. He beat fellow future servicemen George Curry and John Knight, who entered as a chimney sweep and baby respectively.

George was thirty when, on 22 February 1911, he married Kilworth-born Charlotte Ann Beasley, a twenty-nine-year-old dressmaker, at St Andrew's. The presents included a wedding cake from Mrs Entwisle of Kilworth House, where George's sister was later in service. The couple initially lived with Charlotte's widowed mother Emma but later moved to High Street (formerly Chapel Street). Marital responsibilities did not prevent George having fun at the coronation festivities in June 1911 when he won the boot scramble race, beating George Ball Jnr and John Knight. Charlotte evidently had musical talent as in 1912 'Mrs George Morris' on pianoforte was among the entertainers mentioned at a concert in the Belgrave Memorial Hall to raise funds for a new piano. She was also active in church affairs. George and Charlotte's son Ronald George was born on 11 January 1913.

In December 1914 George was among six village men reported to have volunteered for the Royal Army Medical Corps and that month George Ball penned a reference for his worker for the military authorities. However, George, like several of his colleagues, was destined for the Army Service Corps where his work skills were in demand. He was thirty-four when he took the oath at Glen Parva on 1 March 1915. Very soon he was sent to Aldershot, where he passed his trade test and became Driver Wheeler T4/065390. That July, while at 310 Company, 33 Reserve Park, he was appointed acting wheeler corporal. On 3 August 1915 George embarked on the troopship Nirvana & Maidan at

George Morris, another Kilworth soldier in the Service Corps

Southampton for the overnight trip to Le Havre. He served in France for the rest of the war and was promoted wheeler corporal in the field on 25 May 1916. George was sent home for fourteen days' leave in October 1916, allowing him to see his mother a few days before her death. There were two more leaves of a fortnight each, one in 1917 and another ten days after the war ended in 1918. In April 1919 he was appointed paid acting wheeler sergeant and finally returned to Britain in June to be discharged the following month.

After the war George served on the committee of Kilworth's ex-servicemen's club and when Ball's were forced to lay off men he found work with W. Ivens, a large timber merchants at Harborough Magna, near Rugby, where he gave long service. Charlotte, who ran a small shop in High Street, died at the age of fifty-five in 1937. George, a staunch member of the church, served in the Home Guard in the Second World War and in retirement he busied himself with gardening and following the fortunes of Leicester City and was a member of the village bowls club and Evergreen Club. He was eighty-six when he died on 1 October 1967. At his funeral at St Andrew's the coffin was draped with the Union Flag and the mourners included fellow Great War men Ted Cheney, George Ball Jnr and Ernie Spiers. George Morris's brothers Bob and Tom both died before him. Although Bob did not serve in the Great War there is no suggestion of shirking. In December 1915 the *Rugby Advertiser* named William Robert Morris among married men who had enlisted in the town under Lord Derby's scheme. Bob was not called up, however. He was a railwayman for fifty years, starting as a porter. He became a signalman and worked for many years at Welford and Kilworth station. He lived with his wife Winifred at Western Cottages, next door to his parents' house. George's son Ron spent his working life in the brewery trade, except for service in the Second World War as a Royal Artillery officer.

T. R. MORRIS

TOM Morris was seven years younger than his brother George and joined the army several months after him. Despite this, he had something of a harder war, with two periods of intense active service in the Northamptonshire Regiment broken by a spell in hospital with a severe gunshot wound. Although he had reason to be proud of his wartime service, independent-minded Tom was never one to show off medals or brag of his army experiences and after he returned to civilian life he was content to devote his energies to doing the best for his family and community with minimum fuss.

Thomas Richard Morris was born on 18 January 1888 and baptised that April. His family background is explained in the previous entry. After attending North Kilworth school Tom did not follow his father and George to Ball's but went to Kettering to become a carpenter for Phillips, a building firm with Kilworth connections that had built the Belgrave Memorial Hall. He also became a retained fireman in Kettering.

Tom married Florence Mary Rainbow at Kettering parish church on 8 April 1912. The bride was from Cogenhoe, near Northampton, as was the future wife of Tom's other brother Bob. Tom and Florence were living in Wood Street, Kettering, when he attested for war service on 12 December 1915 shortly before the close of Lord Derby's scheme for volunteers to register. Aged nearly twenty-eight, Tom was initially put on the reserve. He was the father of a two-month-old daughter Joan by the time he was mobilised on 15 August 1916, joining the Northamptonshire Regiment in the county town as Private 27421. After training he was sent to France that November, crossing from Folkestone to Boulogne on the 24th, about three weeks after his mother's death. He was kept at the depot in Etaples until he was sent to join the 7th (Service) Battalion near Lens on a wet 8 December. The 7th had been formed at Northampton in 1914 as part of K3, Kitchener's third New Army. Most of its early members were sportsmen who joined up in the spirit of camaraderie fostered on football and other playing fields. Local rugby international Edgar Mobbs rallied friends and admirers to form one company. Heavy casualties on the Somme had diluted the 'pals' character of the battalion by the time Morris arrived at the front among forty-four men under the command of three second lieutenants. A major inspected the new draft next day and the soldiers were issued with anti-gas respirators and shown how to use them.

The battalion was positioned to the left of the Canadian forces who would later seize Vimy Ridge in an epic attack. During December the Northamptons rotated between forward lines and reserve positions as they relieved, and were relieved by, the 2nd Leinsters in trenches made increasingly uncomfortable by rain, snow and cold. On 22 December the battalion's front and support lines were shelled by the Germans. But on Christmas Eve Morris and his comrades were relieved by the Leinsters and next day they were issued with plum pudding, sausages, oranges, apples, bloaters, cigars and beer. New Year was less cheerful. On 30 December the battalion was sent back into the line to relieve the Leinsters in trenches where the mud was three feet deep in places.

In January 1917 the weather continued to compete with the Germans in making the battalion's life a misery. There was sleet, snow and frost while the Northamptons' front and support lines twice came under heavy artillery and trench mortar fire. But later in the month the men were able to use the divisional baths in the village of Les Brebis and go to a cinema showing a film of the 1916 Somme battle. Then the battalion went back into the line where, on 23 January, it had to fight off an enemy attack. At 3am the Germans started a heavy bombardment, chiefly with trench mortars, then sent over an eighty-strong raiding party. One German officer and twelve men leaped into the Northamptons' trenches but the officer and five of the men were killed and the others driven off. The battalion suffered four killed and twelve wounded, mainly in the preliminary bombardment.

On 11 February the battalion set off to rest billets way behind the lines at Lapugnoy, west of Béthune. En route they were inspected by Field Marshal Douglas Haig, commander-in-chief of British forces in France. Morris and his pals had their time taken up with PT and training in bombing and bayonet fighting. The battalion's team also started its successful campaign in the brigade football competition. On 24 February 1917, the day the team beat the 9th Royal Sussex Regiment 12-2 in the semi-final, Morris was stricken with myalgia (muscle pain) severe enough for him to need the attention of the field ambulance and to be excused duty for more than two weeks. By mid-March Morris was back in the lines with his comrades at Souchez, near Vimy, again with the Canadians on their right. The German artillery had been causing casualties among the Northamptons when, on 28 March, Morris was shot in the right shoulder and left arm. It was a fairly severe wound. Morris was treated by the field ambulance and moved to a casualty clearing station. By 1 April he was being cared for at the No 1 Canadian General Hospital in Etaples and was on a ship back to Britain about twelve days later. It meant he narrowly missed his battalion's part supporting the Canadians as they launched their victorious assault on Vimy Ridge on 9 April.

Thomas Morris with a wound stripe on the cuff of his uniform

Morris was cared for at the 2nd Southern General Hospital in Bristol, from where he was granted ten days' leave starting on 25 August 1917. It was perhaps during this break that Tom was walking in civilian clothes in Kettering when an unthinking woman presented him with a white feather, the symbol of rebuke for men suspected of dodging army service. She may have had second thoughts about her gesture had she known Tom was recovering from a wound and was due to return to his regiment as soon as he was fit. At the end of October he was posted to the 3rd (Reserve) Battalion, then on garrison duty at Chatham. The battalion provided drafts for the regiment's other battalions during the war. On 3 December Morris again made the trip from Folkestone to Boulogne. This time he was sent on to the 5th (Service) Battalion, formed at Northampton in August 1914. The battalion's primary task was pioneer work, providing night working parties in the front line. But it frequently tangled with the enemy and suffered 1,581 casualties in the war. When Morris joined the battalion on 10 December it had just been involved in defending positions near Péronne on ground hard won since the Somme battle the previous year. It was soon moved to new duties near Béthune, a few miles from where Morris had served with the 7th Battalion. There, in villages such as Nouveau Monde, Sailly-sur-la-Lys, Estairs, and Laventie, the 5th was employed from the end of 1917 into January 1918 on repairing the parapets and firesteps of trenches, mending wire, improving machine-gun posts and making forms for the concrete components of pill boxes. On 10 March, while the battalion was working in and around Sailly-sur-la-Lys, Morris suffered an accident to his right foot. The records do not specify what happened but the mishap was serious enough for him to be sent back to hospital and it kept him out of the line until the following month.

Meanwhile the Germans launched their great spring offensive and the battalion was rushed by buses to Albert where it sustained casualties as it took part in efforts to hold up heavy attacks. Towards the end of April Morris was back on duty with a battalion hard at work constructing defences, digging trenches, laying duckboards and generally cleaning up in lines north-west of Albert. On the 30th some of the battalion's men took part in an attack by 37th Infantry Brigade while others dug communications trenches despite a German counter-attack.

Thomas Morris (front, fourth from left) at a Bristol hospital

Next day Morris and his comrades were in bivouacs near Hédauville, about four miles from Albert. That night all companies were sent out in support of the 37th Infantry Brigade to consolidate the line captured the previous night. But before work could begin the Germans attacked the captured positions. The Northamptons stood to until 3.30am when they returned to bivouacs. Three other ranks had been killed and eighteen wounded. On 2 July the battalion again prepared to carry out the consolidation work. But even before the men could leave their bivouacs the Germans attacked and regained the whole of the captured line. Around this time Morris was wounded, though apparently not seriously enough for him to be taken off duties.

Reorganisation at divisional level saw the battalion moved by bus and train to various billets north and south of Amiens until, after periods of rest and training, it marched into trenches at Franvillers, south-west of Albert, on 2 August. Within a week it had supported two successful infantry attacks with its pioneer work. On 10 August the battalion started the perilous task of laying wire in front of the lines and several men were wounded. By then the Germans were in retreat, their great offensive having run out of steam. On 5 September two companies of the battalion were sent to mend bridges across the Canal du Nord to facilitate a British advance. Soon the Northamptons were on the move again and on 22 October they marched to billets at Landas, south-east of Lille. With the end of the war in sight, the men's time was taken with clearing up, re-equipping and resting. On the eve of the Armistice they moved into billets at Bon-Secours, on the Belgian border, a little further east. Armistice or not, on 11 November all the battalion's companies were at work on bridges and roads with the Royal Engineers. Four days later Morris was sent home for two weeks' leave. He returned to France to find the battalion still repairing roads. In January 1919 the men prepared a football ground for a divisional race meeting and erected grandstands for the event. The last of the transport horses and mules were sent back to the base at the end of March but Morris still faced more service before he could finally return home. On 2 April he was one of sixty men under two officers who were sent to Avion, outside Lens, for duty with 358 Prisoner of War Company.

He was posted back to Britain on 30 April 1919 ready to be discharged the following month. The joy of being reunited with his family was shattered the following year when his daughter died of diphtheria. Tom and Florence also had sons Eric and Douglas, both of whom were to serve in the RAF in the Second World War.

Between the world wars, Tom worked as a carpenter and joiner for Judkins, a firm that made and refurbished the hefty skittle tables found in most Northamptonshire pubs in those days. When the company closed Tom worked as maintenance carpenter for a shoe firm where he stayed until he retired. He continued to make skittle tables at home as a sideline until demand fell, perhaps as a result of the increasing popularity of darts. The Great War left Tom a legacy of trouble with his 'trench legs', as he called them. In his spare time he enjoyed watching local cricket. Tom Morris's home was at Burghley Street, Kettering, when he died in hospital on 19 October 1956.

G. NEAL

NOTHING has come to light about the life and war service of G. Neal. The widow of Mark Hampson *(see M. Hampson, The Fallen)* was a Neale, although the spelling Neal also appears. The Carter brothers (see this chapter) had Neal relations and Amos Neal was a farmer in North Kilworth around the time of the Great War. But it has not been possible to find a link between any of these and G. Neal.

F. J. OXLEY

THE memorial at North Kilworth bears the names of three Oxley boys – and boys is the apt description. Frederick, the oldest, was not of an age to join the army until more than half way through the Great War and his brothers Leonard and Sidney were still only eighteen and sixteen respectively at the Armistice. However, both younger brothers joined the Royal Navy as boys while the war was still on and so their names were honoured with Frederick's.

The three were the sons of James Oxley, a railway signalman originally from Milton, Northampton, and his wife Ada, also from the Northampton area. Frederick James Oxley was born on 9 November 1898 at Thrapston, the small Northamptonshire town where his father was then working. By 1900 James had transferred to Welford and Kilworth station, where he was to work for the next forty years. The family lived in a house behind the signal box for years before moving to Cranmer Lane.

On 20 March 1903 Frederick started at North Kilworth school where his education was to be interrupted by a couple of bouts of illness. Then, when Frederick was nine, Leonard barely eight and Sidney six, the family was overtaken by tragedy. The boys' mother died on 5 September 1908 after infection set in following the birth of her fourth son Howard on 12 August. Ada Oxley was only thirty-four. A church magazine paid tribute to her as a 'pattern wife and mother' who had taken her sons regularly to the Sunday children's services. James, left with a young family to care for, must have found it difficult to cope. It appears his burden was eased a little by Frederick going to live with relatives. The youngster is recorded as leaving the school and village in April 1909; certainly early in 1911 Frederick was staying with his uncle and aunt at their farm in Rothersthorpe, Northamptonshire. His father had remarried towards the end of 1909 and the following year James and his new wife Mary Elizabeth White, originally from Blisworth, had a son Francis Richard.

Frederick's service during the Great War is said to have been with the Worcestershire Regiment, The Queen's Own Cameron Highlanders and Royal Artillery. He was possibly with the Worcesters when, in December 1917, he was based at Manningtree, Essex. As one of the Kilworth men to receive a gift parcel from the village for Christmas that year, he wrote in his letter of thanks, 'I am sure it is very good of the people of North Kilworth to think about us especially of me, considering that I have not lived there for so long. I hear that Harry Stock *(see H. R. Stock, this chapter)* has gone to France and I wish him the best of luck, I should think there is hardly any young fellows left at North Kilworth now. There is a fellow in our Company who used to live at South Kilworth so I am able to talk things over with him. When I joined up I did not know a single fellow in the regiment and I found it quite an agreeable surprise to see a fellow who had lived so near to my home.'

Frederick emigrated to America in 1922. He did not return until 1946 when a reunion photograph highlighted the Oxley family's fine record of wartime service. Frederick, Sidney and Leonard posed with Howard, who served in the Royal Navy during the Second World War. Also in the picture were their half-brothers Dick and Arthur, who were also in the Second World War, as a naval gunner and a company sergeant major of the Warwickshire Regiment respectively. The group was completed by Cyril Wilson, husband of the Oxleys' sister Edith. He, too, saw wartime service in the Royal Navy. Frederick, who did not marry, returned to California and died on Christmas Day 1975. The brothers' father James, who worked past retirement age as a travelling signalman during wartime staff shortages, died aged eighty on 14 November 1954. His widow died on 5 March 1963, aged eighty-five.

L. W. OXLEY

THERE was nothing of a nautical nature in the Midlands village of North Kilworth to tempt a lad into a life at sea. But Len Oxley, like his younger brother Sid, forged a successful career in the Royal Navy and served in two World Wars.

Leonard William Oxley, second son of James and Ada, was born in Kilworth on 19 August 1900. His family background is detailed in the previous entry. On 11 September 1903 he was admitted to the village school, where he remained until he took the exam for his labour certificate on 7 March 1913. By 1915 he was earning £1 6s 8d (£1.33) a month as a servant for the Entwisles at Kilworth House. Though age exempted him from call-up, sixteen-year-old Len exchanged a footman's livery for naval uniform when he enlisted as a 'Boy II' on 24 October 1916. His early postings included the

Oxley brothers at a family reunion in 1946: (rear, left to right) Dick, Howard, brother-in-law Cyril Wilson and Arthur; (front) Sidney, Frederick and Leonard. All had seen war service

shore training establishment HMS Ganges at Shotley, Suffolk. On 31 May 1917 he became a signal boy and he was serving in HMS Neptune when his engagement as a fully-fledged sailor started on his eighteenth birthday in 1918. He was promoted leading signalman in 1925 but the following year bought himself out of the navy for £24 for reasons unspecified. However, Len rejoined in the 1930s and at some stage served in the Royal Yacht Victoria and Albert. In the Second World War he was mentioned in dispatches while chief yeoman of signals in the aircraft carrier HMS Argus during the North Africa campaign. Len was married twice. His second wife Win was a farmer's daughter and the couple, who had a daughter Mary, lived in Welford. Len, who worked on the buses and also as a die caster, died on 2 June 1982.

S. G. OXLEY

BORN at North Kilworth on 27 July 1902, Sid Oxley had the distinction of being the youngest of the Great War men named on the village memorial. He was the third son of James and Ada Oxley and was baptised Sidney George at St Andrew's on 24 August 1902. His upbringing mirrored that of his elder brother Len, subject of the previous entry. Sid started at the village school when it reopened on 9 September 1907 after the summer break. He appears to have been a responsible pupil and when he was eleven he was one of three children appointed to supervise class monitors, checking for untidiness. He was examined for his labour certificate in December 1914. It is not known what Sid did after leaving school. However, perhaps inspired by Len joining the Royal Navy, Sid became a Sea Scout and in late 1917 he was based at the coastguard station at Rottingdean, near Brighton, watching for enemy ships. Acknowledging receipt of his Christmas parcel from the village, fifteen-year-old Sid wrote, 'There is nothing that makes one feel happier than the thought that he is not forgotten by those at home. This Christmas will be an unhappy one for many, and our brave men are still fighting and dying for us, but I sincerely hope that before many months are out this terrible war will be over.'

The war, however, was not over by the time Sid followed his brother in enlisting in the Royal Navy on 20 August 1918. He was sent to the training establishment HMS Ganges, became a signal boy on 5 February 1919 and, like Len before him, his engagement started from his eighteenth birthday. After the war Sid served in some of the navy's most famous warships including Iron Duke, Admiral Sir John Jellicoe's flagship at the Battle of Jutland. He was also in the super-Dreadnoughts Barham and Queen Elizabeth, and Marlborough, a battleship towed into port after being torpedoed at Jutland. Sid became a leading signaller on 1 December 1925. Again like Len, he served in the Royal Yacht Victoria and Albert. Sid later recalled seeing the young princesses Elizabeth (now the Queen) and Margaret on board. He also served in the Second World War and was promoted lieutenant. He was made an MBE for distinguished services during the war in the Far East and later served in Malta. Sid and his Scottish wife Mabel had a son and daughter who took their respective christian names. After the war Sid worked at Gourock on the Firth of Clyde and died in a home for naval veterans at nearby Greenock on 10 July 1991. Family members recall him as a 'real gentleman'.

Believed to be Percy Packwood

Harry Pallett in Masonic apron

P. W. PACKWOOD

AS a servant in the best households, Percy Packwood knew the importance of a smart turnout when he joined the army. However, an immaculate uniform was no defence against enemy shells and Percy was invalided out with wounds only fifteen months later.

Percy William Packwood was born in North Kilworth on 25 April 1890, the second of four children of William and Sarah Packwood. William was a butcher who was about to take over as landlord of the Swan Inn. The licensed trade was a natural progression for him; his wife was the daughter of James Shave, who ran the White Lion before Henry Spiers took over, and William's own parents William senior and Elizabeth had been at the Shoulder of Mutton for many years. Percy was baptised at St Andrew's on 18 May. He attended the village school where, in 1895, he was absent with his elder sister Annie and brother George for many weeks after they contracted scarlet fever. Percy's other sister Emma was still a baby.

Percy was ten when he took part in an entertainment by the Boys' Bible Class in the schoolroom in February 1901. In a play called *The Magic Horn* he had the part of a fairy disguised as a beggar. A year later he was one of the three stars of *Urchins We*, a sketch for a children's concert. Percy played a bootblack, with his lifelong friend Ernie Spiers as a match-seller and John Dorman as a newsboy. The young trio were all to serve in the Great War. Young Percy had a fair singing voice and at another concert in 1902, to raise funds for the building of the Belgrave Memorial Hall, he gave a rendition of *The Last Little Thing The Baby Said*. He also became a member of the village's minstrel troupe. When Percy was seventeen his family was overtaken by tragedy. In the space of four days in December 1907 his married aunt, eighty-five-year-old grandmother Elizabeth and finally his mother Sarah all died. Sarah, aged fifty-three, had succumbed to pneumonia. Her husband remarried in 1910.

It is uncertain when Percy started in domestic service but in 1911, the year his brother George emigrated to Australia, he was one of two footmen (among fourteen servants plus a governess) employed by Captain Francis Forester at Saxelby Park, near Melton Mowbray. Old Etonian Forester, of the 3rd Hussars, was twice master of the Quorn hounds and fearlessly rode his steeplechasers across High Leicestershire at a pace that astonished all in the field. Percy was working in London when, on 9 September 1915, he went to the Duke of York's Headquarters in Chelsea to join the 1/18th Battalion of the London Regiment (London Irish Rifles) of the Territorial Force. Rifleman 3917 Packwood embarked for Le Havre from Southampton on 2 January 1916, narrowly missing entitlement to the 1914-15 Star.

On 30 January he joined his battalion at Loos, the French mining town which gave its name to the previous September's battle in which the London Irish had fought as part of 141st Brigade of the 47th (London) Division. Apart from a heavy bombardment by the Germans on 3 February, Percy had a quiet first few days at the front. On 16 February he and his comrades were put on a train to Lillers, about sixteen miles behind the lines, and they marched in a gale to Raimbert where they spent the rest of the month resting, training and taking part in route marches. The battalion moved again to various training areas and was at Bruay on 12 March when Percy's problems with a hammer toe meant he was sent back to the base depot. It was 17 May before he rejoined the battalion, which was then in brigade reserve in billets at Maisnil Bouché, a village north of Arras. He would be with his comrades for only five days. On the 20th the battalion moved into the line at a location called Cabaret Rouge on the Arras-Béthune Road. Next day the enemy started a bombardment at 3pm and attacked at 7.45pm. At 2.10am on the 22nd A Company launched an unsuccessful counter-attack after which two officers and thirty-five other ranks were missing. The rest of the day was quiet and most of the battalion was relieved at 9.30pm. At some stage that day Percy suffered a shell wound to his arm and hand. The injury was sufficiently serious for him to be sent back to England, where he arrived on 28 May. He was discharged from the army on 2 December 1916 and later received his Silver War Badge. Percy was also granted a weekly pension of 18s 9d (94p) while out of work. By 1920 he was employed in a household in exclusive Eaton Place, London SW1. Percy, who never married, is thought to have continued in domestic service, becoming a butler. Later he returned to his native village and worked for the Entwisles at Kilworth House. Percy died aged seventy-seven on 10 March 1968 at the home of his sister in Northampton.

F. PALLETT

TWO Pallett brothers gave sterling service in the British Army before, during and after the Great War. Duty done, Fred and Harry returned to civilian life but died about a year apart, both relatively young. They were the sons of George Pallett, a blacksmith born in Wigston Magna, Leicester, and his wife Susannah. The couple were living in North Kilworth by the 1870s though they seem to have moved to nearby Walcote for a while.

Fred, thirteen years younger than Harry, was born at North Kilworth on 25 June 1887. He was baptised Frederick John on 7 August, his christian names honouring a brother he never knew. Seventeen years before Susannah had given birth to twins, naming them Richard Alexander and Frederick John. However, both died of convulsions, after seven and eight days respectively. (Five of Susannah's twelve children died young; she lived to the age of ninety-four.) By the age of thirteen Fred was a farm labourer but found time to appear in the concerts and sports that were such a feature of village life. He appeared in sketches for the Boys' Bible Class show of February 1901 as Polly Flinder and as a soldier. Fred took second place in the two hundred-yards race for over-seventeens at the 1905 flower show sports and in 1910 he performed in a charity evening of musical and dramatic entertainment in aid of a village invalid. Fred, who gave up farm work to follow his father as a blacksmith at Ball's, was sufficiently outgoing to be called on to act as MC for a social at the Belgrave Memorial Hall in February 1913. On 8 April that year, twenty-five-year-old Fred married Eva Mary Walden, a gardener's daughter aged twenty-four in her home village of Creaton, Northamptonshire.

The couple made their home in Kilworth and their first child Edwin was born in 1914. That year Fred decided to join the army. Whether he was influenced by the example of his brother Harry *(see next entry),* a long-serving regular soldier, is not known. Fred joined the Royal Field Artillery as Shoeing Smith 43419 Pallett. His enlistment must have come at least some weeks before war was declared on 4 August because he was sufficiently trained to be sent to France about two weeks after that date. Details of his service have not come to light but he was promoted shoeing sergeant and later quartermaster sergeant. Fred, whose father died in 1918, remained in the army after the war while his wife and son lived in Back Street, Kilworth. But early in 1920, when he was posted to India, he is thought to have taken his family, including new baby daughter Eva Jean, with him. In 1923 he was initiated into a Masonic lodge in Rawalpindi. Freemasonry was fairly common in the British Army in India. Harry was also a Mason, as was another brother Thomas, who had left Kilworth and eventually ran a successful business in London.

Fred left the army later in the 1920s and, again like Harry, opted for the licensed trade, taking over as landlord of the Axe and Compass in the Northamptonshire village of Ringstead. He was only forty-four when he was stricken by acute pancreatitis and died in hospital on 1 January 1932. Fred had another older brother Ernest and sisters Florence and Elizabeth, the latter keeping a shop in Kilworth at some stage.

H. PALLETT

THE lengthy service of some older Great War soldiers was obvious from the orange, blue and red ribbon of the Queen's South Africa Medal. One such veteran of the Boer War was Harry Pallett, whose return home to Kilworth from the veldt is the subject of this book's opening narrative.

Harry was born on 20 March 1874 at Walcote, where his parents George and Susannah were living at the time *(see previous entry)*. He was baptised at Misterton, in which parish Walcote lies, on 18 April. The family, who had earlier lived in North Kilworth, moved back there and Harry was enrolled at the village school. At the age of eight the scholar was at loggerheads with his teachers. Harry was punished for defying instructions to stay behind one evening in July 1882, the latest in a series of misdemeanours. Harry's parents, felt by the school to be encouraging his disobedience, withdrew him and sent him to Husbands Bosworth school instead. The scamp who seemed to find school discipline irksome was later to thrive under the much harsher regime of the Victorian army. Harry was eighteen and working as a baker when he enlisted at Warwick on 7 November 1892. He was sent to Chester as Private 3999 of the Cheshire Regiment and remained in Britain with the 2nd Battalion for the next six years, progressing until he was promoted sergeant on 24 April 1899. By then he had already signed to extend his term of service from the original seven years to twelve. Sergeant Pallett, whose peacetime service included such humdrum achievements as gaining a cooking certificate at Aldershot in 1896, was about to become involved in some serious soldiering. Britain was anxious to have a united South Africa, with its immense reserves of gold and diamonds, as part of the Empire. The Boers, farmers of Dutch extraction, wanted their Transvaal and Orange Free State republics out from under the imperial yoke. By September 1899 the British garrison was being heavily reinforced. Harry was already on a troopship for South Africa when the war started on 11 October.

He had recently undergone mounted infantry training at Aldershot and it was in this role that he fought in South Africa. The Cheshires and other regiments contributed men to mounted infantry companies that travelled with a minimum of equipment wagons so they could gallop in pursuit of the highly mobile Boers if the opportunity arose. Each man carried across his shoulder a bandolier of .303 ammunition for his Lee-Metford rifle, another bandolier round his waist with perhaps a third round his horse's neck. Pallett was with Major General John French's cavalry column when, on 15 February 1900, it relieved Kimberley, the diamond town besieged by the Boers since soon after the start of the war. He was also a member of the forces under Field Marshal Lord Roberts when Johannesburg was taken on 31 May. Harry was present when the Boers were defeated at the Battle of Diamond Hill on 11-12 June in an action that General Ian Hamilton later reckoned had been the turning point of the war. The mounted infantry then rested in Pretoria until 7 July. Harry was later involved in operations around the south-east corner of the Orange River Colony. As in previous wars, disease took a greater toll on the British troops than enemy action and Harry was stricken by peritonitis and enteric fever. He spent many weeks in hospital at Norvals Pont, in Orange River Colony. In December 1901 he embarked for England but not quite in time to spend Christmas at home. He was later awarded the Queen's South Africa Medal with five clasps marking his service. Back from a war that was still in progress, Harry was feted as a hero on his arrival in North Kilworth. Harry was posted for home service with the 3rd Battalion and on 29 March 1902 he wed Mary 'Polly' Alexander in church in Manchester. His new marital status did not affect his commitment to the army for he signed on to extend his engagement to twenty-one years and at New Year 1903 he was promoted colour sergeant. In 1909 he was posted as acting sergeant major to the Cheshires' Territorial 1/4th Battalion where he remained for four years. After breaking his ankle Harry decided it was time to take his pension and left the regiment on 4 February 1914 with twenty-one years and ninety days of service completed. He took with him a long service and good conduct medal to go with his Boer War medal and a military character assessment of exemplary.

The ex-soldier and his wife took over the Waterloo Hotel at Taddington, Derbyshire, but Harry Pallett had not finished with the army. Even though he was forty when the Great War started Harry thought he could still be of use to his old regiment and signed on with the 8th (Service) Battalion of the Cheshires at Birkenhead on 9 September 1914. He remained for only thirty-five days. Harry was discharged as medically unfit while with the battalion at Draycott Camp near Swindon, Wiltshire. The records do not explain whether he had suffered a flare-up of his peritonitis but, whatever the complaint, he was well enough to answer the call of duty yet again when his old CO from the 1/4th Battalion got in touch a few weeks later.

Colonel W. H. Bretherton had come out of retirement to command a proposed new Cheshire Regiment battalion of 'bantams', recruits previously shunned by the army as too short but who were otherwise of adequate build and fitness. The battalion was the idea of Alfred Bigland, MP for Birkenhead East, who headed the local recruiting committee. He had been told of a young man who was rejected by the sergeant at the recruiting office for being an inch below the minimum 5ft 3in. The would-be recruit offered to fight any man in the office to prove his worth and was seen out only with difficulty. Kitchener agreed when the MP sought permission to raise a battalion of men between 5ft and 5ft 3in tall with reasonable chest measurements. Miners from Lancashire and diminutive Cockneys were among those who flocked to join Bigland's Birkenhead Battalion, later the 15th (Service) Battalion of the Cheshire Regiment, when recruiting opened at Birkenhead town hall on 30 November.

Harry was granted a temporary commission on 22 November 1914 and took up quartermaster duties. It is believed he went to France with the battalion early in 1916 but was invalided home. Harry was unfit for much of 1917 and on 21 October that year he was transferred to the Royal Flying Corps as a captain and quartermaster. A medical board the following month decided he was not fit for general service but could serve at home or on garrison duty in a warm climate abroad. In fact he served with the RFC at Harlaxton, near Grantham, Lincolnshire. At Christmas of 1917 he wrote to Rector Cox from there to say, 'May the time not be far distant when the church bells of North Kilworth are ringing out the glad tidings of Peace and Goodwill.' Like everyone in the RFC, Harry transferred to the new Royal Air Force on 1 April 1918. He dispensed with his uniform for the last time in about May 1920 when he left No 13 Group RAF.

He and his wife then kept the Davenport Arms, a pub at Calveley, near Crewe, Cheshire, where customers included boat folk from the nearby Shropshire Union canal. Harry Pallett was fifty-eight when he died in January 1933, weakened by the peritonitis that had struck him as a young soldier in South Africa. As a sad postscript to his story, in 1940 Harry's widow Mary failed in attempts to obtain a pension based on his time with the RAF although she was in straitened circumstances due to ill-health. Apparently Harry's service was reckoned insufficient.

W. T. PEBODY

A KIND and helpful character dedicated to farming and his beloved homing pigeons, Billy Pebody was not obvious warrior material. Defective eyesight from birth also might have been expected to rule him out of army service. However, in 1916 a pleasant demeanour and minor disability were no bar to a young man joining up. Billy was nothing if not dutiful and he spent more than three years in khaki.

He was born in North Kilworth in 1896, son of William Thomas Pebody, farmer and parish clerk, and his wife Drusilla. The infant was given both of his father's christian names when he was baptised at St Andrew's on 10 January 1897. William started at the village school on 10 May 1901 and continued there until he was twelve, leaving on 23 July 1909 with George Stock *(see G. W. Stock, The Fallen)* and Will Cheney *(see A. W. Cheney, this chapter).* Other future soldiers were among the lads with whom William played football in the field behind his home on the corner of The Green. William joined his father working on the family farm and, encouraged by relatives and Cecil Spencer, who farmed at The Grange, he developed a lifelong interest in pigeons.

Billy had to leave the birds in the care of his parents when he joined the army. He went to attest at Market Harborough on 7 December 1915 and, aged nineteen, he was called up into the Sherwood Foresters (Nottinghamshire and Derbyshire Regiment) on 30 January 1916. Young Pebody, whose father also had sight problems, was not going to become a crack marksman with his poor eyes and was destined not to be sent abroad. On 7 February 1917 he was transferred to the 25th (Works) Battalion of the Durham Light Infantry as Private 57338. The battalion became part of the Labour Corps that April. He was later transferred to 411 Agricultural Company with whom he served until his discharge in 1919.

Billy, then twenty-two, went back to working on his father's farm. On 7 August 1922 he married Ethel Pinfold, a twenty-one-year-old domestic servant, at St Peter's, Dunchurch, near Rugby. He took over the running of the farm at about the same time. Billy and Ethel had a daughter the following year but she did not survive infancy. The Pebodys settled into a routine of hard work, which did not prevent Billy playing a full part in village life. He followed his father as church sexton, was a chorister, bell-ringer, member of the ex-servicemen's committee, a parish councillor, charity trustee and long-

Billy Pebody (rear, far right) at a wedding. The date is unknown

Billy Pebody and his wife Ethel tending their cows at Kilworth

time member of the Oddfellows. He remained a pigeon-fancier all his life and specialised in the Muff Tumbler breed. He won prizes in leading shows at Olympia and Crystal Palace and exported specimens all over Britain and abroad. As a founder member of the Muff Tumbler Club, he was a renowned judge and regular contributor to *Fur and Feather* magazine. In the Second World War the old soldier was kind to the Italian PoWs sent to work on his farm, giving them cigarettes. But Bill Pebody could show toughness when it came to fighting for his principles, particularly if the interests of his home village were at stake. He battled remorselessly in the early 1950s to prevent land held under the local Town Land Charity being sold off.

The Pebodys, who specialised in dairy cattle and poultry, gave up working their sixty-acre farm in about 1961, never having had a proper holiday in all their married life. Billy quit the parish council in 1964 after more than thirty years. Typical of the man was a letter he sent to the *Harborough Mail* in 1965 after there had been complaints about pigeons causing a nuisance in the belfry at St Andrew's. Openings in the tower were sealed, depriving the birds of winter shelter. Billy wrote, 'This harsh treatment is not warranted where pigeons are concerned when one remembers the number of servicemen's lives these little creatures saved from 1914 to 1918.' To his satisfaction a fancier took some of the birds into his care. William Thomas Pebody was seventy-four when he died on 8 January 1971. Ethel died on 23 May 1987. Relatives still have the silver matchbox given to Billy after the Great War. It contains a 1916 silver coin, said to be the 'King's shilling' handed to him when he signed on for the army.

H. T. PEBODY

BORN in North Kilworth on 10 January 1900, Harry Pebody was still only eighteen when the Armistice was signed and was therefore one of the youngest men named on the village war memorial. He was the only son of Joseph Henry Pebody, farm worker and sometime gardener at Kilworth House, and his wife Mary Alice. The couple took their boy to be baptised Henry Thomas at St Andrew's on 22 April. Harry, who had three sisters, started at the village school on 13 March 1903 at the same time as fellow infant David Dorman *(see D. I. Dorman, this chapter)*. He appears to have been a willing scholar as he won a prize for regular attendance in 1908 to go with the Sunday school prize he received from the Rector the year before. He was king to Gwennie Phillips's May queen in 1912 and the pair were carried to Kilworth House on one of Governor Ball's carts for the celebrations. Unfortunately, by the end of the month Harry was off school with measles.

Family tradition has it that Harry enlisted in the Great War under age but it is not known with which regiment he served. However, it may be that he was a Private 60200 Henry T. Pebody known to have been in the Royal Warwickshire Regiment. After the war Harry worked felling trees. On 1

October 1921 he married Katie Mildred Denton, from Moulton, Northampton, who was in service, and they set up home in North Kilworth. When the village's ex-soldiers held their annual supper at the White Lion in November 1922 Harry was there to give a song accompanied by Ernie Spiers on piano. Harry and Katie later moved to Moulton where their first child Irene was born in January 1925. The couple had six more children, of whom two daughters and two sons survived infancy. One son served in the RAF for twenty-seven years, retiring as a warrant officer.

Harry Pebody in later years

Harry worked in Moulton for the local Co-op for some years, delivering bread and milk around Overstone and Sywell. He later drove a coal lorry and worked for a Northampton building firm. Harry served in the Home Guard during the Second World War. Ill-health kept him out of full-time employment after the age of fifty-six but Harry, always respected as an honest and hard worker, took on tasks such as sweeping chimneys and sharpening saws to support his family. Known as Harry Pep, he was a keen gardener who specialised in growing dahlias and did not like to venture out without one of his blooms as a buttonhole. Henry Thomas Pebody died suddenly at Moulton in February 1979. It is believed he was a relative of William Pebody *(see previous entry)*. Through some aberration in the alphabetic ordering of names on the war memorial, Harry's follows that of William.

V. PERROT

A MID the army uniforms at the postwar fete for North Kilworth's servicemen Victor Perrot stood out in the distinctive cap and jacket of a Royal Air Force flight sergeant. Photographs of the event give the impression of a smart, confident yet cheerful chap.

Victor Leon Abel Perrot was born on 12 September 1890 in Brighton, Sussex. His father was an auctioneer who rejoiced in the name Charles Ferdinand de St Clair Perrot, providing a rather obvious clue to the family's Gallic origins. But although Perrot ancestors included a French judge, Charles was born in south London like his wife Mary Anne, née Davis. Victor had an elder sister Vivienne. Early in the twentieth century the family was still living in Brighton and Charles had become manager at a mineral works. After school days Victor took a job as a clerk for the London and North Western Railway Company and in 1911 was living in a boarding house in Islington, London. At some stage he moved to the Midlands, perhaps encouraged by someone more senior in the company. Possibly as early as 1914, he was living in North Kilworth as a lodger at Mrs Packwood's house. The obvious inference is that he was a clerk at Welford and Kilworth station but perhaps he worked further afield for the LNWR, for instance at the mainline station at Rugby. While he was at Kilworth, some of his washing and mending was undertaken by Lily Phillips (later Spiers), who charged him two shillings (10p) in 1915 for running up a couple of nightshirts.

Twenty-five-year-old Victor's railway career was interrupted when he enlisted in the Royal Flying Corps on 10 January 1916 with the rank of 2/AM. He was promoted 1/AM five months later and corporal on 1 March 1917. In January 1917 Victor, until then ground-based, started having flights as a passenger in biplanes such as the Avro, FE2b, DH6 and RE8. He appears to have been stationed in the south of England as two of the sorties involved swoops over the Isle of Wight. Victor took to the air only six times that year, with his last flight in September, so it seems unlikely that he was being groomed seriously as a pilot at that time. Promoted flight sergeant at the beginning of 1918, Victor resumed flying and was shown stalls, spirals, loops, vertical dives and 'low stunting'. He took partial control of an Avro for the first time on 4 August. The last entry in his flying logbook was two weeks later so if Victor was aspiring to become a fully fledged pilot his hopes were

Victor Perrot in November 1915 before he joined the RFC

dashed. By then the Royal Flying Corps had vanished into the newly formed Royal Air Force with which Victor served until he was transferred to the reserve on 17 April 1919.

Victor was living at Kilworth again when, on 1 September 1921, he married twenty-four-year-old Dorothy Dimblebee, daughter of grocer Albert Dimblebee, of Husbands Bosworth. Dorothy's younger sister Marjorie later married Bill Clarke *(see W. T. Clarke, this chapter)*. Victor and Dorothy, known as Dolly in the family, spent their married life in Rugby where Victor continued working as a railway clerk. He also gained certificates in signalling and block telegraph regulations and worked at Coventy at some time. The couple had no children. Victor was a churchgoer, talented pianist and keen gardener who kept himself fit by swimming and playing tennis. He never drove but cycled everywhere. He was in the Home Guard from June 1940 to December 1944. Victor Perrot was ninety when he died in St Cross Hospital, Rugby, on 8 November 1980. Dorothy died in 1982.

Victor Perrot with Dorothy while on leave from the RFC

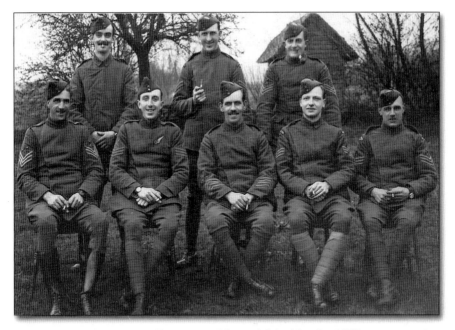

Victor Perrot (front, second from right) with other NCOs

A. J. PITCHER

A VOLUNTEER rifleman during the Great War, Alec Pitcher was also a farmer, naturalist, gardener and poet. He was the elder son of Harry and Louisa Pitcher. Harry, agent for an agricultural society and sometime shoemaker, shopkeeper and farmer, was a leading member of North Kilworth Band and for years he and his violin-playing brother Alf were in demand for musical events in the village. Harry's father Reuben, also a shoemaker and grazier, was born in South Kilworth but had moved to North Kilworth where he lived with his wife Dorcas and became a member of the parish council.

Alec, born in North Kilworth on 22 March 1892 and baptised Alec James at St Andrew's on 19 April, had a younger brother Cecil and sisters Ida and Madge. Two other sisters died as babies. Alec started at the village school on 21 September 1896 and remained there until June 1904 when he left at the same time as Alf Stapleton, another future soldier. Alec went to work on the land, probably with his father, and was still living at home before the Great War. While perhaps not quite so dedicated to music as his father and uncle, he played the cello well enough to join Alf at the Belgrave Memorial Hall in February 1912 when there was an entertainment to raise funds for a new piano. That July, at the annual flower show sports, he took third place in the two hundred-yards race and second in the mile.

Alec must have volunteered for the army fairly early in the war because on 21 July 1915, when he was twenty-three, he was sufficiently well trained to be sent to France with the Rifle Brigade. Details of his service have not emerged but he was a good enough soldier to rise to the rank of sergeant, with the service number S1537, by the end of the war. He wrote to North Kilworth in December 1917 from the Voluntary Aid Detachment in West Bromwich but whether his presence at that medical establishment indicated he was wounded or ill is not known. After the war Alec returned to live with his parents in High Street where, by then, they were running a shop. However, after the death of Reuben in 1920, Harry took his family to live at Fearn Farm at Allexton in east Leicestershire, near the Rutland border. Alec concentrated on poultry farming and advertised to say that day-old chicks and ducklings were a speciality. In 1923 he married Violetta Woodhouse, a coal merchant's daughter, in the parish church of her home village, Cholsey, near Wallingford in Berkshire. Violetta was only thirty-seven when she died in hospital on 12 August 1927. Alec was still farming when, the following year, he married Alice Lilian Hawksworth in church at Thornton, near Market Bosworth.

Harry died in 1942 and Alec and his wife later left the farm to live at Glaston in Rutland. The couple had moved to nearby Uppingham by the time Alice died in 1956. Alec won scores of show awards for the vegetables and flowers, particularly dahlias, that he grew. A member of the British Naturalists' Association, he was also an expert on mosses and spent years amassing a collection of five hundred species. His book of poems, *A Carpet of Moss,* was published in 1967. Alec died, aged seventy-seven, on 4 January 1970. His funeral was at Glaston church. Nearly forty years after Alec's death the Rutland Horticultural Society was still presenting the A. J. Pitcher Cup for the best dahlias.

Alec Pitcher, rifleman and later a farmer, naturalist and poet

H. SHARP

FOR years Horace Sharp was content to lead a peaceful life dedicated to farming and his beloved angling. But his limp was a clue to the fact that, as a young man, he had been among the first to volunteer for war and suffered the consequences.

Horace was born in Lutterworth on 17 August 1889, the third son of Harry and Mary Ann Sharp, née Masters. The couple had eight children, two of whom died young. Horace was baptised at Lutterworth parish church on 6 October 1889. Harry was a grazier at the time Horace was born but he later became a beer agent working from home in Station Road, Lutterworth, and early in the twentieth century he took over the Coach and Horses pub in Church Street in the town. Horace, who trained as an engineer, courted Elsie, sister of the North Kilworth brothers Frank and Walter Morley *(see F. C. and W. J. Morley, this chapter)*. When war broke out he was determined to volunteer as soon as possible but decided it was best for him and Elsie to marry before he was called away. The couple bought a licence, thus avoiding the delay of having banns read, and wed at St Peter's in Rugby, where Elsie was then living, on 1 September 1914. Horace was twenty-five, his bride a year younger. It was a brief honeymoon; Horace enlisted four days after the ceremony.

He joined the Royal Engineers, with the regimental number 47238, and eventually rose to sergeant. Horace landed in France on 11 September 1915 and served with 97th Field Company. His service records have not survived but at some stage Horace was badly wounded in the head and leg and captured by the Germans. It is believed German doctors treated his head injury by inserting a plate. His leg injury left him with a limp for life. The incident when he was wounded possibly came during the German spring offensive of 1918 for Horace had written to North Kilworth on 11 January that year to say, 'I am in the best of health and still going strong.' Unfortunately he put no address on his note. Before the war ended Horace was released under prisoner-exchange arrangements and was discharged from the army on 15 November 1918, four days after the Armistice. The Sharp family had not escaped tragedy during the war. Horace's elder brother Frank, aged twenty-nine, had died of wounds on 15 November 1917 while serving as a private with the Essex Regiment in Egypt. Frank, who had married in 1915, is named on Lutterworth's war memorial. His grieving father died in February 1918, leaving Mary Sharp to run the Coach and Horses until the early 1920s.

The Sharp family in Lutterworth in 1910. Brothers (rear, from left) Frank, Horace,
William and Albert. Their sister Ethel is between parents Mary and Harry;
brother Ernest is at the front

Horace and Elsie Sharp got married soon after war was declared

Horace and Elsie lived at her parents' home, Highwayside on the South Kilworth road, from where Horace farmed until he retired in the late 1950s. It is understood he served in the Home Guard during the Second World War. Horace is recalled as a quiet, patient and reserved man who loved nothing better than to go off on fishing trips. A regular visitor at Highwayside was Horace's fellow Great War soldier Ernie Spiers *(see E. Spiers, this chapter)*, who would stroll from his home in Western Cottages for a chat. Horace suffered ill-health in the last years of his life and was seventy-four when he died on 13 June 1964. Elsie died ten years later.

T. F. SMITH

IN 1918 Thomas Francis Smith was listed as a North Kilworth voter absent from the village by reason of naval or military service. The following year he was living back in Cranmer Lane but, by the early 1920s, he appears to have left the village. Unfortunately, further details have not been found.

G. C. SPENCER

FARMER'S son George Cecil Spencer was born on 22 January 1896 at Halse, a hamlet near Brackley, Northamptonshire. His father, George Hilton Spencer, and mother Annie, née Lawrence, appear to have moved around their native Northamptonshire as their elder son John Lawrence was born in Earls Barton about four years previously. However, by the twentieth century the couple had settled in North Kilworth, farming from their home on The Green. Both sons attended the village school for a while, although George left at the age of seven to attend a private school. Education completed, John and George both helped their father who, by the Great War, was farming at The Grange on the Leicester Road. No details have emerged of George's war service – John appears not to have joined up as he is not named on the village memorial. George returned to continue working on the farm, eventually taking over at The Grange from his father. He and his wife Gladys had two daughters in the 1930s. George, who later farmed near Towcester, Northamptonshire, died on 22 August 1970.

E. SPIERS

A FINE tenor and accomplished pianist, Ernie Spiers was always much in demand. His talents graced the church choir, musical events at the Belgrave Memorial Hall and Saturday night sing-alongs in the pub. His skill as a painter and sign-writer also made him a highly regarded employee at Ball's. Ernie's contributions to village life continued for decades, interrupted only by his time in the army during the Great War.

Ernest Spiers was born on 26 February 1890 in Twycross Street, Leicester, son of Henry Spiers, a warehouseman in the hosiery trade, and his wife Harriett, née Bradbury. The couple already had daughters Bertha and Nellie. The family moved to North Kilworth in the early 1890s when Henry took over as publican at the White Lion, which he would run until the mid 1920s. His son showed an early talent for entertainment. In January 1902 eleven-year-old Ernie played the part of a match-seller in *Urchins We*, a sketch for a children's concert in the schoolroom. His abilities seemed to stretch to athletics for that August he won the fifty-yards race for his age group at the flower show sports. Later Ernie joined pal Percy Packwood as a junior member of the village's minstrel troupe. By his early twenties his repertoire for village concerts included songs such as *I Don't Care If There's A Girl There* and *Love Makes The Whole Year June*. Ernie started courting Lily Phillips, whom he had known from childhood, and bought her an ebony brush and comb and handglass for her twenty-first birthday in 1911. Lily, born in Kettering, Northamptonshire, was the daughter of George Phillips, whose firm built the Belgrave Memorial Hall. But from the age of two she was brought up by her grandparents Thomas and Elizabeth Phillips at Western Cottages along the road from the White Lion. Thomas, a wheelwright, was a workmate of Ernie at Ball's.

Some village men had already joined up by the time Ernie and other future soldiers Arthur Whyles and Charlie Dunkley contributed to the entertainment at the annual social and dance in the memorial hall on 14 January 1915, when the room was patriotically decorated with bunting and flags. Ernie's mother died that March. He and Lily, who worked as a dressmaker in the village, were both twenty-five when they were married by Rector Cox on 14 August 1915. Ernie enlisted in the Army Ordnance Corps on 25 October and was home for six days' leave the following February. Made lance corporal in May 1916, Ernie was stationed at Devonport, Plymouth, and Lily stayed in the area for six weeks in September and October that year to be near him. She was also there in December 1917 when Ernie, by then a corporal, wrote to Kilworth to thank villagers for the Christmas parcel they had sent. Acknowledging his luck in not being sent abroad, he said, 'I cannot grumble. I have been very fortunate staying in England so long.'

After the war the couple settled in at Western Cottages, where they would spend the rest of their lives. Their daughter Doris was born in 1921. Ernie returned to Ball's where he was known for the perfection of his lining and writing work on carts. Army service had not dulled his appetite for singing. In April 1923 he performed at a social to raise funds for ex-servicemen and sang a solo in church for harvest thanksgiving that autumn. On the eve of Armistice Day 1923 the ex-servicemen held a supper in the Belgrave Memorial Hall and, after the solemn toast to The Fallen, Ernie entertained them with *Pack Up Your Troubles In Your Old Kit Bag*. His humorous songs and piano-playing were a feature of the annual event when it moved to the White Lion.

Ernie was with Ball's for forty-five years then from 1951 he worked at United Dairies by Welford and Kilworth station. But well into his retirement in the 1960s he would do the odd job lining a trap for Ball's or sign-writing on vehicles and preparing coffin plates for undertakers. Ernie, a chorister for forty-two years, played the piano on Saturday nights at The Swan in Kilworth, or as far afield as The Windmill in Gilmorton. In later years he sang or played the accordion to entertain Kilworth's Evergreen Club where he and Lily, a former Sunday school teacher, were members. Fifty roses from Gandy's, the local growers, marked Ernie and Lily's golden wedding in 1965. They were the village's oldest married couple when they celebrated their diamond wedding in 1975 at the village hall where Ernie had entertained so often.

Ernie Spiers died on 13 December 1976, aged eighty-six. Lily lived only a few weeks more, dying on 29 January 1977. The couple are buried in the churchyard of the village they served so long and well.

Ernie Spiers with his wife Lily. They were married for 61 years

J. H. SPRIGGS

AGED forty when he enlisted in the army in 1915, James Spriggs was Kilworth's oldest volunteer of the Great War. (Paul Kenna VC and Harry Pallett were older than Spriggs but Kenna was a career officer and Pallett a former regular soldier who rejoined.) Whether James felt obliged to join up to honour the memory of his younger brother Albert *(see A. Spriggs, The Fallen),* who had died of wounds in Belgium, can only be a matter for speculation. Whatever his motivation, he gave valuable service which led to him being awarded the OBE after the war.

James Henry Spriggs was born on 11 November 1874 at Haselbech, Northamptonshire, where his father James was a farm labourer. James senior, originally from Walcote, near North Kilworth, had married Annie Chambers the previous year. The couple also had a daughter Annie and were living in Welford when Albert was born in 1880. By 1901 James senior was widowed and working as a wagoner on a farm at North Kilworth. That year James Henry was a railway stoker and boarding at an address in Cambridge. By 1915 he had became a railway driver at British Thomson-Houston whose Rugby factory had its own lines and locomotives. That March word reached Kilworth of his brother's death. On 10 December 1915 James joined up in Rugby.

A medical revealed that the 5ft 11in recruit had varicose veins in both legs but he was passed fit for garrison duty at home or abroad. James became a Royal Fusilier with the regimental number G/21710. However, he was soon transferred to the Royal Engineers as Pioneer 128199 and was sent to France on 8 March 1916. He joined his unit, No 3 Battalion Special Brigade, four days later. His duties included handling supplies of the gas that had become a much feared weapon used by both sides in the Great War. James was with his battalion for six months until he was shot in the upper left arm on 7 September 1916. He was treated at Steenwerk before being sent to England via hospital in Boulogne a week later. He was transferred to a reserve company while he was treated at the 5th Northern General Hospital, later the site of Leicester University. His wound was not serious enough to warrant him being discharged and in 1917 he was based at Wearde Camp in Cornwall and elsewhere. He had eighteen days in hospital that March and April suffering from lumbago. After facing several travelling medical boards he was sent to take part in perilous duties at the Royal Engineers Experimental Station at Porton, north of Salisbury, Wiltshire. This was a secret establishment opened in 1916 for testing chemical weapons. It grew into a large hutted camp where agents such as chlorine, phosgene and mustard gas were assessed. James wrote to Kilworth from No 4 Hut at Christmas 1917 to thank villagers for the parcel they sent containing an 'excellent' cake and pie. Acknowledging that he had spent much time working away from Kilworth before the war, he said, 'It is a pleasure to me to know that I have such kind friends in the village, considering that I am quite a stranger to you all.' Like so many soldiers that year he expressed the wish that everyone would be home for the following Christmas. It was, in fact, February 1919 before James was demobbed, his war wound having being judged for pension purposes as leaving a ten per cent degree of incapacity.

James lived in Church Street after the war. On 19 October 1920 he went to County Hall, Warwick, where the Lord Lieutenant, the Earl of Craven, presented him with the OBE. The award was for 'conspicuous courage in connection with very dangerous experimental work in a poisonous atmosphere, often causing great physical discomfort and ill-health'. James returned to work as an engine driver. He was forty-eight and living in Bristol when he married Emma Holyland, twenty-one-year-old servant daughter of blacksmith Charles Holyland, at Kilworth church on 20 August 1923. After the ceremony conducted by Rector Cox the bride placed her bouquet of red and white carnations on the war memorial in memory of James's brother.

The couple, who had no children, stayed in Bristol for a while. But they were living in South Kilworth when James, by then sixty-nine and retired, was accidentally killed. He was found dead from head injuries on the road between South and North Kilworth on the evening of Saturday 21 October 1944. James had evidently been knocked down by a passing vehicle but it was never traced. The funeral was at North Kilworth on 25 October. Recording an open verdict at the inquest the following month, the coroner called for a clampdown on speeders to end the 'slaughter' on the roads.

A. STAPLETON

ALFRED Stapleton was born in North Kilworth in 1892 and baptised at St Andrew's on 20 March that year. He was a son of George Stapleton, a farm labourer and wagoner, originally from Kings Cliffe, Northamptonshire, and his wife Dorothy. The couple were living in Kilworth by 1891 when both were twenty-seven.

Alf attended the village school and was among pupils who earned a mention in the local press for taking part in concerts there in 1902 and 1904. In June 1904 Alf passed his labour certificate ready for leaving school. His family twice suffered tragedy while he was a youngster. In 1902 his brother Robert had died at the age of fifteen, then in 1906 his seventeen-year-old sister Emma died suddenly. Before the Great War Alf laboured on a farm and in his spare time was a member of the village's football team and band. In 1913 he gained a second place with his roses at the annual flower show, evidence of gardening skills that would prove useful in later life. Details of Alf's war service have not come to light although it is possible he was in the Army Service Corps. After the war he worked driving an oil tanker lorry. He was twenty-nine when, on 7 September 1921, he married Mary Philomena Archer, thirty-two-year-old daughter of a dairy farm worker from Little Hay, near Lichfield, Staffordshire. The ceremony was at Holy Cross Catholic chapel in Lichfield.

The couple lived in High Street, North Kilworth, in the 1920s at which time Alf was chairman of the village's ex-servicemen's club and acted as master of ceremonies at social events for the club and other organisations. He later worked as a gardener for Colonel Hew Belgrave and Miss Viola Belgrave in Kilworth. By then he and Mary, also known as Daisy, were living at Stoney Cottage near the church. During the Second World War Alf joined the Home Guard. However, he was dogged by ill-health and died on 9 September 1945 at the age of fifty-three. At his funeral, attended by representatives of the Home Guard and British Legion, the coffin was draped with the Union Flag.

H. R. STOCK

THE years 1917 and 1918 brought anguish and cruel uncertainty for the Stock family. It was torture enough for parents William and Minnie that they should lose their soldier son George, struck down by influenza before he could even leave the country *(see G. W. Stock, The Fallen)*. The grieving couple had to contend also with the constant anxiety of having their younger son Harry serving overseas with the infantry. However, Harry did survive the Great War to spend his working life as a railway signalman like his father.

Harry Stock was born at North Kilworth on 30 September 1898 and baptised by Rector Belgrave that November. His second christian name was Rainbow, his mother's maiden name. Harry was only three when he started at the village school on 18 October 1901. He appears to have enjoyed his time there and also earned prizes for best attendance in his class at Sunday School in 1907, 1909 and 1910. On 5 October 1911 he passed his labour certificate to leave school but it is not known when he followed his father and brother into railway employment.

George Stock died in February 1917 and it was probably later that year that Harry was called up, becoming Private 39503 in the 1st Battalion South

Harry Stock (rear, third from right) in South Staffs Regiment

Harry Stock after being moved to the Royal Munster Fusiliers

Staffordshire Regiment. The Staffords were sent to the front in northern Italy in November 1917 to take part in one of the partly forgotten episodes of the war. They were in the 7th Division among British troops needed to bolster the Italians, whose forces had been routed at Caporetto (now Kobarid in Slovenia) by German-backed Austro-Hungarian forces. Harry wrote home on 29 December 1917 (his letter does not say from where) to say how he enjoyed the contents of the village's gift parcel when he arrived back in billets on Christmas Day after a few days of trench-digging. He added, 'Our Commanding Officer gave us a good Xmas Dinner on Boxing Day so on the whole I have had a fairly good time, but hope to be among you all for the next.' By the time he sent home a postcard dated 15 April 1918 the Staffords were being relieved by the Manchester Regiment at Asiago on the edge of the Dolomites. However, Harry was then attached to a garrison battery of the Royal Munster Fusiliers in the area. The Staffords were still in northern Italy at the end of the war but it is uncertain when Harry was discharged. In early 1919 he was still listed in North Kilworth as an absent military voter.

He eventually returned to live with his parents in Church Street where he remained until his wedding. Harry was a twenty-nine-year-old railwayman when he married blacksmith's daughter Nellie Goude at the parish church in her home village of Great Brington, Northamptonshire, on 12 May 1928. Harry ended his railway career as a signalman and his home was in Crick, Northamptonshire, when he died aged seventy-two on 27 February 1971.

J. H. SUTTON

AMONG the older soldiers named on the war memorial, James Henry Sutton was born on 13 September 1877 at Newton, near Rugby. He was the son of Henry Sutton, a farm labourer and later shepherd, and his wife Sarah Ann, née Goodson. The couple, who had many Sutton relations in the Warwickshire village, had eight children in all and the family lived in a cottage on a lane leading to Swinford, across the border in Leicestershire.

Jim worked as a farm labourer before the Great War. He was nearly thirty-seven when the war started but it is not known when he joined the army. Jim, who is thought to have served in the Warwickshire Regiment, was on leave when he married thirty-four-year-old Mary 'Polly' Sturgess at St Mary's, Clifton, near Rugby, on 2 September 1918. Mary, a labourer's daughter from North Kilworth, had worked as a domestic servant. She and Jim settled in Kilworth after he left the army. Jim served on the committee of Kilworth's ex-servicemen's club and worked at British Thomson-Houston between the wars. Jim Sutton was living at Green Lane, Kilworth, when he died aged seventy-six on 24 February 1954. Mary died in February 1962.

**Fun on an outing to Blackpool pleasure beach for (rear from left) Jack Ormond, ?,
Alf Stapleton, Jim Sutton; (front) George Ball Snr, Cecil Brooks and Albert Simons**

F. J. WEARING

THE Wearings are the sixteenth and final example of a family with more than one son named on the Great War panels of the memorial at North Kilworth. Frederick James and Francis Leonard were the sons of Kilworth-born farm labourer William Wearing and his wife Sarah Ann, née Reynolds, originally from Great Bowden, near Market Harborough. Their surname often appears spelt Waring.

Frederick, the elder brother, was born at Kilworth on 27 October 1879 and baptised at St Andrew's in August 1882. He was nineteen and working as a bricklayer when, on 4 July 1899, he married Birmingham-born servant Louise Bale at the register office in Coventry, where both were then living. By 1911 the couple had two sons and two daughters and were living in Nuneaton, Warwickshire, where Frederick worked as a timber wagoner. Details of his war service are not known.

F. L. WEARING

WILLIAM Wearing had found a new job labouring on the railway by the time his son Francis Leonard was born on 13 April 1893. The Wearings were living in South Kilworth at the time but soon returned to North Kilworth where they lived on the Rugby road until well after the Great War. Their son, baptised at St Andrew's on 24 November 1895, was given the names of a brother who had died in 1892 aged eleven months.

Francis, usually known by his second name, started at the village school on 26 June 1896. As a twelve-year-old in December 1905 he was severely reprimanded with Allen Cheney for failing to return to lessons after being allowed out to watch the hounds. On 28 September the following year he passed his labour certificate to leave school, but not before coming second in the hundred-yards race for boys of his age group at the annual flower show. In 1911 he was a house porter at the East India United Service Club in St James's, London, where another future soldier from Kilworth, Edward Carter (*see E. W. Carter, this chapter*), was working. Nothing has emerged about his war service.

A. T. WHYLES

THE talents of Arthur Whyles as a cricketer, gardener and musician were highly respected in North Kilworth before the Great War. And, to the village's benefit, army service did nothing to dim his enthusiasms. Arthur Thomas Whyles (the surname was often spelled Whiles at the time) was born on 2 April 1881 at Thurlby in the Lincolnshire flatlands near Bourne. His father John was a farm labourer, married to Sarah, née Downs. Arthur had two elder brothers, two elder sisters and younger brother.

The family later moved to Hoby, near Melton Mowbray, but by 1901 John had taken a job as a shepherd at North Kilworth where he, Sarah and their younger children lived near the church. Arthur worked for Rector Cox as a gardener, an occupation he would follow for the rest of his life, war service excepted. His younger brother Herbert was then an apprentice painter. On 18 November 1903, Arthur married Annie Spriggs at St Andrew's. The bride was the daughter of James Spriggs and sister to Albert and James

Henry, who were both to fight in the Great War. The couple's son Percy was born the following year and daughter Phyllis followed in 1908.

Arthur was a member of the football and air rifle clubs and the brass band. He played cornet and handbells and earned a press mention with his rendition of *Oh Oh Antonio* in a minstrel troupe concert at the Belgrave Memorial Hall in January 1909. Arthur and his pal Norman Maddison, who lived at North Kilworth mill, were good runners at a mile and half-mile. It is said that at the annual horticultural show sports the pair had a pact to each win one race while the other balked a rival runner from Husbands Bosworth. Meanwhile Arthur's vegetables regularly won awards fair and square at the show. His onions, beans, carrots and potatoes all took prizes at the event on the eve of the Great War in 1914. That December, thirty-three-year-old Arthur and his brother Herbert, who had wed in 1912, were among six married men from Kilworth said to have put themselves forward for service in the Royal Army Medical Corps. As has already been noted, some were eventually accepted by other branches of the army. But first, Arthur and Annie suffered two blows early in 1915. Their daughter Phyllis died aged six in February. Then the following month word arrived that Annie's brother Albert *(see A. Spriggs, The Fallen)* had died of wounds in Belgium. Arthur eventually joined the Army Veterinary Corps and, as Private SE/20257, he was sent abroad, possibly to Salonica. His father died in 1916.

After the war Arthur, who lived with Annie in Church Street, again immersed himself in village life. At village entertainments in the 1920s he acted as master of ceremonies or played the cornet. Guests at a Ladies Hockey Club social in 1922 had to guess the weight of a thirty-two-and-half-pound pumpkin grown by Arthur.

But his greatest delight was cricket. Arthur had not been out of uniform long when he helped form a boys' cricket club with himself as secretary and coach. He was also groundsman and captain of the village club, which played in the Lutterworth League. Kilworth's cricketers sang, 'We are A. Whyles's army, A. Whyles's men are we, We cannot bat, we cannot bowl, What earthly use are we?' The words, belted out to the tune of *The Church's One Foundation,* were based on the infantry song *We are Fred Karno's Army.* (Karno was a music hall impresario famous for slapstick acts.) Arthur, one of the ex-servicemen who gave the war memorial a regular spruce-up, later moved to Yelvertoft, Northamptonshire. He died there aged eighty-seven on 14 May 1966.

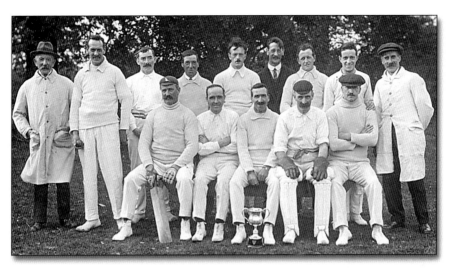

Cricket team in 1925: (rear from left) Bill Packwood, Frank Howkins, George Ball Snr, Len Carter, ?, Jim Howkins, Cecil Brooks, – Cook, Herbert Allsopp; (front) Norman Maddison, ?, Arthur Whyles, Tom Whiteman and Herbert Bennett

C. WIFFEN

THE identity of C. Wiffen remains a mystery. The name has not shown up in any documents relating to North Kilworth around the time of the Great War. The village, however, deemed him to have close enough connections to the community to warrant inclusion on the war memorial.

ANOTHER WAR

P IP, Squeak and Wilfred. The names of comic strip characters in the *Daily Mirror* were applied irreverently to the 1914 or 1914-15 Star, the British War Medal and the Victory Medal. Whether proudly displayed or stored half-forgotten in a drawer, these medals were the nation's tangible recognition of a Great War soldier's service. However, the rewards most returning servicemen desired were a return to steady work, ideally with a gradually improving standard of living, and no more war. As we know, it did not happen that way but demobilised soldiers could not foresee the deprivations of the Depression or the rise of Nazism. Neither could they anticipate that, some twenty-one years after their return home, they would see another generation off to war while they themselves often donned uniform again as members of the Home Guard.

Whatever their hopes for the future, North Kilworth's former soldiers inevitably had a bond based on their wartime experiences. They formed North Kilworth Ex-Service Men's Social & Sports Club, with a shilling (5p) annual subscription. One of the club's more ambitious outings was a trip to London on Saturday 19 August 1922. The old comrades watched the Changing the Guard ceremony and paid homage at the Cenotaph in Whitehall and at the tomb of the Unknown Warrior in Westminster Abbey. They later went to St Paul's and the zoological gardens in Regent's Park and fitted in a theatre visit before arriving home at 3.30am on Sunday. Each Armistice Day the men assembled at the memorial where they were met by the Rector and churchwardens. A wreath was laid and a short prayer said before the group marched to the church to join other parishioners for a service.

Inevitably, smaller local ex-servicemen's groups faded away as the British Legion, founded in 1921, could tackle welfare matters with the authority of a national organisation. A representative attended the Kilworth comrades' supper in November 1926 to explain the Legion's history and aims. A Husbands Bosworth and District branch was formed the following year, its area including Kilworth. The branch's initial membership of thirty-two rose to more than one hundred by 1930. But at first Kilworth's club continued its annual outings to such destinations as Great Yarmouth and was still holding social events into the 1930s.

This book is chiefly concerned with the Great War and it is not necessary to detail here the events of 1939-45. Suffice to say that, as a global catastrophe, the Second World War dwarfed the first; total civilian and military deaths are put at a minimum sixty-one million. German bombing meant that civilians in Britain were effectively on the front line. On the night of Thursday 14 November 1940, North Kilworth's villagers gazed at a western sky aglow from the flames of the blitzed city of Coventry a mere eighteen miles away. However, Britain's 326,000 military deaths represent fewer than half the number for the Great War, a fact confirmed by a casual glance at the lists of names on virtually any village war memorial.

In 1948 Mrs Whiteman, driving force behind the erection and maintenance of Kilworth's memorial, agreed that responsibility for its care should pass to the parish council as most of the original trustees had died or left the village. At the annual parish meeting on 30 March 1950 Ron Hancock, a veteran of the Second World War, proposed that the names of all villagers who had served in that conflict should have their names added to the memorial. The idea was raised again in September 1951. It is not certain how many names were involved but perhaps it was decided that it would be impracticable to contain all on the memorial. That idea and a proposal to move the cross to a more central position on the green fell into abeyance. In 1952 it was decided to add the names of the four men who had died and as elegant a solution as possible for accommodating them was worked out with masons Allsopp and Sons, of Market Harborough. It involved replacing two of the memorial's eight panels with new Hopton Wood stone tablets. The wording of the first tablet now reads: To The Glory Of God And In Memory Of Men Of This Parish Who Fell In Two World Wars. Under the heading 1914-19, the first six names of the Great War fallen follow, now in alphabetical order and without mention of rank. The final three Great War names are on the second tablet. The Second World War names are listed below them under the heading 1939-45.

**Home Guard with Great War veterans George Ball (front, far left),
David Dorman and Charlie Carter (both front, far right)**

The other tablets naming the Great War soldiers who returned needed no alteration. Allsopp's bill for fixing the tablets and cutting the new names was £22 16s 10d. (£22.84) and money also had to be found for concreting work around the base. About £18 was taken from money originally intended to provide treats for Second World War servicemen and £5 was found in the Great War ex-servicemen's funds. There was a few shillings shortfall and the parish council clerk was told to settle the amount and charge it on his expenses.

Here are the stories behind the names from the Second World War.

A. E. T. BARTLEY

THEY called her the Mighty Hood. The largest warship in the world when she was commissioned in 1920, the battlecruiser HMS Hood was the pride of the Royal Navy and a symbol of imperial strength in the inter-war years. When, on 24 May 1941, she was blown up and sunk by the German battleship Bismarck the news was greeted with profound shock in Britain. In North Kilworth the grieving had a local focus. The family of Arch Bartley, one of the 1,415 crewmen who died, lived in the village, having moved there at the invitation of friends to escape the bombing in Portsmouth.

Archibald Edward Thomas Bartley was born in Portsea, Portsmouth, on 24 May 1903. He was the first child of Archibald and Elizabeth Bartley, née Mear, who were then in their early twenties. Archibald senior, originally from Brixton, south London, was a cooper for the Royal Navy. He and Elizabeth, from Portsea, went on to have two more sons and a daughter. Young Archibald attended the naval school at Greenwich before entering the Royal Navy as a boy shortly after the end of the Great War. He trained at the shore establishment HMS Ganges in Suffolk where he was marked for accelerated advancement. On 27 April 1920 he became a signal boy in HMS Barham. Arch, only 5ft 3in, was serving in that super-Dreadnought when his engagement proper started on his eighteenth birthday in 1921. His superior ability as a signaller was regularly noted as he served in various warships in the 1920s. At some stage he became friends with North Kilworth sailor Sid Oxley *(see previous chapter),* who was ten months older and had trained at Ganges a few months before him. The two served together several times, including in Iron Duke in 1923 and 1924. On 13 October 1923 Arch married Mabel Davies, who was from an army family, in Portsmouth. In later years the couple were invited by Sid Oxley to take holidays at Kilworth.

In the 1930s Bartley served in the cruiser Suffolk in the East Indies and Canal Zone and immediately before the war was instructing at Ganges. He was teetotal, a member of Toc H (a fellowship with origins in the Great War) and a keen cricketer. A story is told in the family of how he once bowled out the opposition in record time, having promised Mabel at tea that his side would not be long finishing. On the outbreak of war he was called back to sea. In 1940, with Portsmouth a prime target for the Luftwaffe, Mabel accepted Sid Oxley's suggestion to go to live in Kilworth, taking her children Bob and Pat. After a while at the Oxley home they moved in with Mrs Holyland and later had rooms at the rectory. By then Arch was a signal boatswain in Hood. About 860ft long and with a displacement of more than 42,000 tons, Hood was still an impressive sight. However, the years had taken their toll and the outbreak of war prevented her being removed from service for the major work needed to bring her up to scratch. In May 1941 Hood sailed with the new battleship Prince of Wales to intercept the modern and fast Bismarck that was attempting to break out into the North Atlantic. The Bismarck and the heavy cruiser Prinz Eugen were shadowed by HMS Norfolk and Arch's old ship Suffolk, which reported the German ships' position to Hood. Shortly

Archibald Bartley (front centre) before the Second World War

before 6am on 24 May Hood and the Prince of Wales opened fire on the Bismarck in the Denmark Strait. The Bismarck returned fire, straddling the Hood with her second or third salvo. The magazine was hit and fire quickly spread. Just after the Bismarck fired her fifth salvo, a huge explosion split the Hood in two, and within three minutes she had sunk. It was Bartley's thirty-eighth birthday. There were only three survivors, the last of whom died in 2008. The Bismarck, damaged in the encounter, escaped but was left unable to manouevre after further attacks by British ships and torpedo aircraft. The German battleship sank on 27 May after being torpedoed by HMS Dorsetshire.

Arch Bartley is named on Panel 45, Column 3 of the Portsmouth Naval Memorial on Southsea Common and in the Hood Chapel, St John's, Boldre, Hampshire. After the war his family continued to live in North Kilworth where Mabel died in September 1970 aged sixty-six.

A. J. COATON

BERT Coaton survived more than four years after the end of the Second World War. However, his time as a prisoner of the Germans had left him with health problems that contributed to his early death and it was considered fitting that his name should be included on the memorial.

Albert John Coaton was born on 26 May 1915 at Stanford, near Rugby. He was one of five children of Charles Coaton and his wife Sarah, née Arnold, who had met while working in service. Charles became a chauffeur after being sent to Daimler in Coventry to learn about motors. He worked for Lord Braye at Stanford Hall and later became chauffeur for John Entwisle at Kilworth House. The Coaton family then lived at Kilworth House Cottages on the Lutterworth Road a mile or two from North Kilworth. Before the war Bert, who was a little over 6ft tall, was an assistant at the Lutterworth drapery store Kimpton Smith.

He enlisted in the Northamptonshire Regiment on 16 May 1940 and was sent for infantry training before being shunted through a series of postings to various regiments. In June he was transferred to a home defence battalion of the Bedfordshire and Hertfordshire Regiment. On 12 August 1942 he was moved to the Royal Ulster Rifles and then, on 25 March 1943, to the 5th Battalion the Royal Inniskilling Fusiliers. He went with the Inniskillings to North Africa on 12 April but before the end of the month was transferred to the 2nd Battalion North Staffordshire Regiment. Coaton was still in North Africa when American and British troops landed at Anzio, south of Rome, on 22 January 1944. German defences were light but the US commander General John Lucas preferred to consolidate his bridgehead rather than advance. Five days later Bert was transferred yet again, ready to play his part in bolstering the Anzio operation. As 5888583 Fusilier Coaton, he became a member of D Company 9th Battalion The Royal Fusiliers, part of 167th Infantry Brigade. He was put ashore at Anzio on 17 February, by which time the Germans had counter-attacked and the Allies had forfeited the chance of a rapid conclusion to the Italian campaign. Coaton was captured by the Germans only a day after arriving in Italy. It is thought a comrade trod on a landmine and Bert caught the blast in the face and was temporarily blinded.

Bert Coaton served in several units before he was taken prisoner

His family were alarmed when letters from him ceased. To add to their anguish, a letter that his sister Barbara sent on 18 February was returned, saying he was missing. Finally the family received a card dated 25 March, sent from the prisoner-of-war camp Stalag VIIA at Moosburg, north-east of Munich. Bert wrote, 'Dear Mum & Dad, Just a few lines to let you know that I am safe and well. I hope that both of you and all at home are also. I was wounded about my face and hands about a month ago. I was discharged from hospital yesterday, my wounds having almost healed. Do not worry. I am OK and hope to see you all soon. Give my love to all, love from Bert.' He was soon moved to Stalag XIA at Altengrabow, near Magdeburg. He wrote to Barbara from there on 10 April, saying he had been to see a concert in the camp and was due to attend a football match.

Bert was repatriated on VE Day, 8 May 1945, and sent to hospital in Hereford. On 30 August he was posted to a selection and training battalion, probably in a sedentary post. He was later sent on sick leave and was finally discharged from the army on 24 May 1946. Bert left with a reference describing him as 'a hardworking, reliable and conscientious soldier who has given every satisfaction in the performance of his duties'. He was awarded the 1939-45 Star, Africa Star (1st Army Clasp), Italy Star, British War Medal and Defence Medal. After the war Bert learnt shoemaking but it was difficult to find work. He lived quietly at the cottage in Hawthorn Road to which his family had moved. Bert, who did not marry, was not one to talk of his war experiences and, although a churchgoer, he preferred not to attend the annual Remembrance ceremony. He did, however, relate how one mate in PoW camp kept an illicit radio hidden in an accordion. Dogged by ill-health, Bert was only thirty-four when he died on 1 March 1950. He was buried at North Kilworth three days later.

A. R. L. HORNBY

NO North Kilworth family lost more than one son during the Great War. So it was particularly harsh fortune that robbed Captain Albert Hornby and his wife Esme of both of their boys in the Second World War, when British combatant deaths were far fewer. Army officer Billy Hornby was shot dead while trying to escape from a German prisoner-of-war camp; his younger brother Mike, a RAF pilot, was killed in a freakish incident thirteen months later.

The Hornbys were from a family of Lancashire cotton magnates who had established themselves as country squires near Nantwich in Cheshire. Billy and Mike's grandfather was Albert Neilson Hornby, a renowned nineteenth century cricketer who captained Lancashire for twenty years. Known as Monkey because of his 5ft 2in stature and energetic displays on the pitch, he also captained England and in 1882 opened the second-innings batting against Australia with Dr W. G. Grace. He captained England at rugby, played football for Blackburn Rovers and rode fearlessly to hounds. The eldest of his four sons, Billy and Mike's father, also captained Lancashire. The youngest son John was famed as Hornby of the North. He turned his back on the family wealth to explore the expanses of northern Canada – with a break during the Great War when he won a Military Cross on the Somme. Jack Hornby and two companions starved to death in a cabin on the Thelon river during an expedition in 1927. Between the wars Albert and Esme Hornby had a home at Killinardrish, Co Cork, where Albert was Master of the Muskerry foxhounds. When the house burnt down they found another home at Ballincollig, Co Cork. In about 1940 the couple also took Ivy House, formerly known as The Billet, in North Kilworth, possibly so that Esme could be closer to her mother in England. By then Billy and Mike were both in the services and rarely if ever visited Kilworth.

Albert Raymond Lonsdale Hornby – why and when he became known as Billy has been forgotten – was born on 17 July 1916 in Clifton, Bristol, though it is unclear why his parents were there. Lonsdale was his mother's maiden name. Billy spent much of his childhood in southern Ireland where he grew to share his father's love of country sports. But in 1925 he was sent to a school called Arnold House at Llanddulas on the North Wales coast. He was thirteen when, in September 1929, he started at Harrow School, like his father and grandfather before him. He had middling success academically, played for his house Druries in the inter-house rugby competition of 1933 and studied economics before leaving in the summer of 1934. Billy spent the following year travelling in France, Italy and Austria and in 1936 went to Trinity College, Cambridge. However, in 1937 he had a car accident, left Cambridge and joined his parents on a cruise to Bermuda. Later that year Billy joined a firm in New York to study American business methods but was not sorry to leave in 1938. He wrote to his mother, 'If I could find an heiress, I wouldn't mind the job.' Billy, who had been in the Officers' Training Corps

Billy Hornby in New York City where he worked before the war

German soldiers at attention as Billy Hornby's coffin passes

Respectful German officer with a wreath for Hornby's coffin

at Harrow, applied in March 1939 for a commission in the 4th Queen's Own Hussars, his father's old regiment (and that of another Harrovian, Winston Churchill). He gave as his occupation 'gentleman of leisure', apparently no bar to acceptance into a smart cavalry regiment. Second Lieutenant Hornby was sent for training at Kandahar Barracks in Tidworth, Wiltshire, where he also found time for polo, and was then posted to Yorkshire. While there in the severe frost and snow of early 1940 he and another subaltern bet they could walk to York and back, a distance of fifty-four miles, in twenty-four hours. They managed the feat with an hour to spare. The war had been on for fourteen months when, in November 1940, the Hussars were sent to Egypt. Billy's fellow officer George Kennard (who became Sir George, baronet and commanding officer of the regiment) recalled how they had one last hunt together in the Shires. Kennard, known as Loopy, wrote in his autobiography that Billy was 'that special friend...with whom I had shared horses, money, girlfriends and good times'. The Hussars and their Mark VIB light tanks sailed from Liverpool, via Durban, to Port Said, from where they drove to Tahag Camp in the desert. General Wavell's British 8th Army had started pushing the Italians back towards Libya and Billy and Loopy went to take a look at the front line.

But no sooner had the Hussars modified their tanks for desert use than they were ordered to Greece where, in March 1941, Britain sent sixty thousand troops to defend the country against German invasion. The Hussars landed at Piraeus and Billy and his comrades then boarded a northbound train, waved off by cheering Greeks. They got off at Veroia in the mountainous country forty miles west of Salonica and continued to move north and west. As part of 1st Light Armoured Brigade, the Hussars faced the first German attack on 6 April and were then involved in a series of rearguard actions as the British withdrew to the south. The Luftwaffe found slow-moving targets on every road. One aircraft tried to machine-gun Billy and Loopy as they clung to a motorcycle on a mountain pass. Billy, promoted lieutenant at the beginning of the year, was captured on 26 April as the Hussars headed for Kalamata in the far south of Greece. His friend John Peacock's troop had become separated from the main squadron while holding off pro-Nazi Greeks. Billy was sent on a motorbike to tell them to rejoin but on the way back they fell into a German trap and were taken prisoner. The rest of the squadron was ordered to surrender three days later after covering the evacuation of British troops.

Billy wrote to his mother from the prison camp in Salonica where he was taken. He said, 'I was with a small party on a motorcycle and got cut off from the rest. Suddenly we found ourselves faced by several machine-guns hidden by the road and were not able to offer any resistance. It was sickening. They have treated us well so far and we have been given some corned beef they captured. Also a little bread from the village. But I have got no equipment with me, no blankets or anything as I had to leave it behind. Fortunately I was wearing my greatcoat as it was cold riding the bike.' He added, 'I shall be all right here so do not worry.' Esme Hornby did not receive the letter until 19 February 1942 and by then Billy had been dead for nine months.

He was shot by guards at about midnight 21/22 May 1941 as he and Peacock tried to escape. They hoped to make it back to their squadron, not knowing of its surrender. The Hornbys were notified of his death in a War Office telegram to Ivy House on 24 July. The Germans provided a guard of honour for Billy's funeral at the British War Cemetery, Salonica, at 11am on 23 May and laid a wreath. The pall bearers were members of his regiment captured during the evacuation. Billy was twenty-four.

George Kennard wrote to Mrs Hornby from a German prison camp, saying, 'The gallant attempt, of which I hope you will be as proud as we are, was in accordance with his bravery shown throughout the campaign, a bravery that aroused the admiration of us all.'

Peacock also wrote to Billy's parents that October in an attempt to provide some comfort. He said, 'I know he felt no pain and the deep feeling of those of the regiment and the sympathy of six hundred Yugoslav officers interned with us would have moved you. He took it as his duty and longing to be free. The chance was so hopeful neither of us considered failure and his only message was "good luck".' At the end of the war Peacock wrote again to give the Hornbys details of the ill-fated escape attempt. He said, 'You will know better than I that his nature would not let him lie down under capture and I can assure you that it was not foolhardiness that took us out that night. I had been out already preparing the way the previous night.

'Although Billy had gone first I also was outside but I honestly believe I could have done nothing to help him. He had penetrated one ring of wire further than me and was already out of sight in the shadow of trees round the Greek barracks which were our prison. We had received every possible aid from our fellows before setting off and they were stunned at the outcome.'

Billy's remains were later reburied at Phaleron War Cemetery, south-east of Athens, where more than two thousand Commonwealth servicemen are buried or commemorated. He lies in grave 9 D 12.

M. G. L. HORNBY

MIKE Hornby won the Distinguished Flying Cross during RAF operations in North Africa at the time of the struggle between Britain's 8th Army and Erwin Rommel's Afrika Korps. His parents' concerns about his safety in such dangerous times naturally were heightened after the death of his soldier brother Billy. Yet Mike did not die in an airborne encounter with the enemy; he was accidentally killed while off duty in circumstances never fully explained.

Michael George Lonsdale Hornby, younger son of Captain Albert and Esme Hornby, was born at South Stoneham, outside Southampton, on 4 February 1918 *(see previous entry for more family background)*. He was first sent to school in West Malvern, Worcestershire, where he was awarded his colours for football. Mike then followed Billy, nineteen months his senior, to Arnold House in Llanddulas. As a ten-year-old he was top of the class in arithmetic, good at drawing but weak in French. There was a break with family tradition when Mike was sent in September 1931, not to Harrow like his brother, but to Pangbourne, the Berkshire college that prepared youngsters for a nautical career. He left in December 1935 with a mate's certificate but for some reason did not pursue a life at sea. Instead Mike went to Kenya to try his hand at farming. He found a six-hundred-acre farm with two hundred cattle for four thousand pounds. He wrote to his mother, 'I have still to buy oxen and a cart but they are very difficult to get these days.' Mike also described how a day's quiet fishing with a friend was interrupted by an angry elephant whose attentions they escaped by shinning up a tree and sitting it out for two hours.

It is thought Mike had learned to fly during a visit to New York and at some stage he decided to join the RAF. He undertook much of his training in Iraq where the RAF had long maintained a presence. By April 1941 Mike was in Egypt as a sergeant in 203 Squadron which flew reconnaissance missions over the Mediterranean with aircraft types such as the Baltimore,

Michael Hornby (front left) with his RAF friends in North Africa

Wellington and Liberator. On 25 June 1941 he wrote to his mother in an attempt to reassure her about not hearing from his brother. He said, 'I should think news of Billy should come through fairly soon, which will be a great relief.' It was August before Mike received a telegram telling him of Billy's death. At the end of that month he was commissioned as a pilot officer and did much valuable work spotting enemy shipping. He managed to visit his farm while on leave but found the experience very depressing because 'the place was dying of neglect'.

Mike was twenty-four when he was killed on 22 June 1942 at Burg el Arab on the Egyptian coast. An Air Ministry letter to his father at North Kilworth outlined the circumstances. It said, 'Your son was one of a bathing party which had picked up what was thought to have been a hollow float. This exploded when the lorry in which the party was travelling reached camp.' The true nature of the 'float' remained a mystery.

Mike's commanding officer wrote to Captain Hornby, 'The place Michael made for himself in the squadron was probably unique in as much as, by his hard work, fine personality and general demeanour, he had endeared himself to all the officers and men. He had carried out some very fine operational flights and, as you are probably aware, was one of the most trusted aircrews. The details of the accident are not clear but I think you can gain some slight consolation from the fact that Mike did not suffer in any way. His death was instantaneous.'

The citation for Mike's DFC, printed in *The London Gazette* on 7 July 1942, said, 'This officer has displayed exceptional courage and devotion to duty. He completed eighty operational sorties. On a recent occasion his accurate report of the movement of an enemy convoy enabled a striking force to make a successful attack.'

Billy and Mike's younger sister Judith was a Wren courier in London during the war. She married an American and went to live in the US. The brothers' parents stayed on in North Kilworth where Captain Hornby died in 1952. His widow Esme moved to Gloucestershire but kept in touch with the village. She died in 1974. Michael Hornby is buried in El Alamein War Cemetery, grave XXIV E 1-2.

*   *   *

IN the years since the Second World War, North Kilworth's memorial has remained the focal point for the village's act of Remembrance each November.

The Great War is now slipping beyond the reach of human memory and the youngest veterans of the Second World War are in their eighties. But as *In Grateful Memory* went to press, Britain was still sending its young men and women to serve, and too often to die, in far-off places. Perhaps this book can stand as a modest tribute to them as well as to those of previous generations. Lest we forget.

BIBLIOGRAPHY

Anderson, Ross. *The Battle of Tanga 1914*. Tempus Publishing 2002

Anon. *The Northamptonshire Regiment 1914-1918*. Reprint. The Naval & Military Press 2005

Beazley, Ben. *Leicester During the Great War*. The Breedon Books Publishing Co 1999

Brighton, Terry. *The Last Charge*. The Crowood Press 1998

Bruce, C. D. *History of the Duke of Wellington's Regiment*. The Medici Society 1927

Bull, Stephen. *The Loyal North Lancashire Regiment 1855-1970*. Tempus Publishing 2002

Corrigan, Gordon. *Mud, Blood and Poppycock*. Cassell 2003

Davies, Frank & Maddocks, Graham. *Bloody Red Tabs*. Leo Cooper 1995

van Emden, Richard. *Boy Soldiers of the Great War*. Headline 2005

Edensor, Dennis. *Wings of the Morning*. Diamond D Publishing 2006

Ensor, R. C. K. *England 1870-1914*. Oxford University Press 1936

Ferguson, Niall. *The Pity of War*. Allen Lane The Penguin Press 1998

James, E. A. *British Regiments 1914-18*. Reprint. The Naval & Military Press 1998

James, Lawrence. *Warrior Race*. Little, Brown 2001

Kennard, George. *Loopy. An Autobiography*. Leo Cooper 1990

McGreal, Stephen. *The Cheshire Bantams*. Pen & Sword Military 2007

Massie, Robert K. *Dreadnought*. Jonathan Cape 1992

Massie, Robert K. *Castles of Steel*. Jonathan Cape 2004

Mead, Gary. *The Good Soldier. The Biography of Douglas Haig*. Atlantic Books 2007

Middlebrook, Martin. *Your Country Needs You*. Leo Cooper 2000

Packenham, Thomas. *The Boer War*. George Weidenfeld & Nicholson 1979

Powell-Williams, Clive. *Cold Burial*. Viking 2001

Spencer, William. *Army Service Records of the First World War*. Public Record Office 2001

Taylor, A. J. P. *English History 1914-1945*. Oxford University Press 1965

Wilson, A. N. *After The Victorians*. Hutchinson 2005

Wylly, H. C. *The Loyal North Lancashire Regiment 1914-1919*. Royal United Service Institution 1933